By
Royal Command

By the same author
Birth of the Few
Forewarned Is Forearmed
The Golden Book of Remembrance

By Royal Command

Henry Buckton

*An Account of Their Service
by Members of the Royal Household
and Representatives of
Her Britannic Majesty Queen Elizabeth II*

Foreword by
Dame Barbara Cartland

PETER OWEN
LONDON & CHESTER SPRINGS PA

PETER OWEN PUBLISHERS
73 Kenway Road London SW5 0RE
Peter Owen books are distributed in the USA by
Dufour Editions Inc. Chester Springs PA 19425-0007

First published in Great Britain 1997
© Henry Buckton 1997

Jacket portrait by Mara McGregor
© Crown Copyright 1997/MOD
Reproduced with permission of the Controller of HMSO

All Rights Reserved
No part of this publication may be reproduced in any form or by any means without the written permission of the publishers

A catalogue record for this book is available from the British Library

ISBN 0-7206-1025-7

Printed and made in Great Britain
by Biddles of Guildford and King's Lynn

*Dedicated to the Royal British Legion
(Patron: HM the Queen)*

Acknowledgements

I should like to thank Sir Kenneth Scott, who (although now retired) was one of the Queen's Private Secretaries at the time that I began my research. When I first had the idea for the book I approached him to find out whether the Palace had any objections. Luckily there were none (if there had been, I could not have continued with the project).

I should also like to thank Penny Russell-Smith, Assistant Press Secretary to the Queen, to whom I have no doubt been a nuisance over the past few years.

Particular thanks go to Dame Barbara Cartland, who was the first person to read the draft manuscript and subsequently wrote the Foreword.

Thanks must go, above all, to those listed below, who – as the reader will see – have in essence written the book by contributing their personal thoughts and memories.

The contributors are the Right Honourable the Earl of Airlie, Sir Hardy Amies, the Venerable Percival Ashford, Vice-Admiral Sir Peter Ashmore, Colonel Sir Brian Barttelot, Colonel Sir Piers Bengough, the Right Reverend John Bickersteth, Sir Roger du Boulay, Captain John G. Canning, Sir Sydney Chapman, the Reverend Canon Alan Coldwells, Dr William Cole, Commander the Right Honourable the Lord Cottesloe, the Right Honourable the Viscount Daventry, Major-General Peter Downward, Admiral Sir Desmond Dreyer, Lieutenant-Colonel John Dymoke, Henry Elwes, the Right Honourable Sir Peter Emery, Sir Martin Farndale, Captain C. A. Farquharson of Whitehouse, Sir Edward Ford, General Sir David Fraser, Lord Gisborough, Andrew Grima, the Reverend Canon Ian Hardaker, Captain

David Hart Dyke, Dr David Illingworth, Sir Malcolm Innes of Edingight, Sir Jack Jacob, the Right Honourable Tom King, the Right Honourable the Earl of Lichfield, Major Sir Fergus Matheson of Matheson, Major Sir Philip Pauncefort-Duncombe, the Right Honourable the Lord Rix, Field Marshal Sir John Stanier, Lieutenant-Colonel Sir Blair Stewart-Wilson and Godfrey Talbot.

I should also like to thank Liane Greyson of Sweet and Maxwell for permission to use an extract from 'The Supreme Court Practice (1995)', written by Sir Jack Jacob QC for *The White Book*. My thanks are also due to Peter Hope Lumley, Public Relations Consultant to Sir Hardy Amies. Sir Hardy's contribution is a combination of new material specially written for this project and material from his autobiography *Still Here* (Weidenfeld and Nicolson, 1984), reproduced with the permission of Sir Hardy Amies.

Foreword

by Dame Barbara Cartland DBE

The title *By Royal Command* conjures up visions of colonial gentlemen and officers in smart red-and-gold uniforms. This book is equally thrilling because it tells us all about the occupations of the gentlemen who serve Her Britannic Majesty in many ways.

The men who have written about their various appointments are all very colourful, from the Lord Chamberlain of Her Majesty's Household to a Member of Parliament, and they have all one thing in common – their devotion to their Sovereign.

They give us an insight into the importance of our Royal Family and what it means to serve them in the fullest sense of the word.

Anyone who reads this book, which I thoroughly recommend to you, will see why we need to keep the pageantry so brilliantly executed in order to thrill our tourists so much.

I loved reading about the quaint customs that go with some of the offices – for instance, where the Constable of the Tower of London is allowed to take any sheep or cattle that fall off London Bridge. Unfortunately, so far he has been unlucky.

Mr Buckton has brought all the stories together brilliantly, and this makes the book compulsive reading.

Contents

INTRODUCTION 13
1 BEHIND THE SCENES: THE ROYAL HOUSEHOLD 17
    The Right Honourable the Earl of Airlie KT GCVO PC JP
        Lord Chamberlain of Her Majesty's Household, 1984–
    Sir Sydney Chapman MP
        Vice-Chamberlain of Her Majesty's Household, 1992–1995
    Vice-Admiral Sir Peter Ashmore KCB KCVO DSC
        Naval Equerry to King George VI, 1946–1948
        Extra Equerry to Her Majesty the Queen, 1952–
        Master of Her Majesty's Household, 1973–1986
    Lieutenant-Colonel Sir Blair Stewart-Wilson KCVO
        Deputy Master of the Household and Equerry to Her Majesty the Queen, 1976–1994
        Extra Equerry, 1994–
    Sir Edward Ford KCB KCVO ERD DL
        Assistant Private Secretary to King George VI, 1946–1952
        Assistant Private Secretary to Her Majesty the Queen, 1952–1967
        Extra Equerry to Her Majesty the Queen, 1955–
    Dr David Illingworth CVO
        Surgeon Apothecary to Her Majesty's Household at the Palace of Holyroodhouse, 1970–1987

2 BY APPOINTMENT TO HER MAJESTY THE QUEEN 36
    Andrew Grima
        By Appointment to Her Majesty Queen Elizabeth II, Jeweller, 1966–1986
    Sir Hardy Amies KCVO
        By Appointment to Her Majesty Queen Elizabeth II, Dressmaker, 1955–

The Right Honourable the Earl of Lichfield
   Royal Photographer
Godfrey Talbot LVO OBE
   BBC Correspondent at Buckingham Palace, 1948–1969

3 DIPLOMACY AT HOME AND ABROAD 53

The Right Honourable Sir Peter Emery MP
   Parliamentary Private Secretary in the Foreign Office, 1960–1963
Sir Roger du Boulay KCVO CMG
   Vice-Marshal of the Diplomatic Corps, 1975–1982
Captain John G. Canning OBE
   Messenger to His Majesty King George VI, 1946–1952
   Messenger to Her Majesty the Queen, 1952–1967
   Superintendent of the Queen's Messengers, 1967–1978
Captain David Hart Dyke CBE LVO RN
   Commander of the Royal Yacht, 1978–1980
Sir Roger du Boulay KCVO CMG
   Vice-Marshal of the Diplomatic Corps, 1975–1982

4 CEREMONIES AND SETTINGS: HISTORY AND HERITAGE 80

Sir Roger du Boulay KCVO CMG
   Vice-Marshal of the Diplomatic Corps, 1975–1982
The Viscount Davidson
   Captain of the Queen's Body Guard of the Yeomen of the Guard, 1986–1991
Admiral Sir Desmond Dreyer GCB CBE DSC
   Gentleman Usher to the Sword of State, 1973–1980
Major-General Peter Downward CB DSO DFC
   Governor, the Military Knights of Windsor, 1989–
The Reverend Canon Alan Coldwells
   Canon of St George's, Windsor, 1987–1995
Sir Malcolm Innes of Edingight KCVO WS
   Lord Lyon King of Arms, 1981

Secretary of the Order of the Thistle, 1981
Field Marshal Sir John Stanier GCB MBE DL
ADC General to Her Majesty the Queen, 1981 – 1985
Constable of Her Majesty's Tower of London, 1990–
Sir Jack Jacob QC
The Queen's Remembrancer and Senior Master of the Supreme Court, Queen's Bench, 1975–1980

5 GUARDS AND BODY GUARDS 103

Sir Martin Farndale KCB
Colonel Commandant, Royal Horse Artillery, 1988
Master Gunner St James's Park, 1988
Major Sir Fergus Matheson of Matheson, Bart
Standard Bearer, Her Majesty's Body Guard the Honourable Corps of Gentlemen-at-Arms, 1993–
Major Sir Philip Pauncefort-Duncombe, Bart DL
Harbinger, Her Majesty's Body Guard the Honourable Corps of Gentlemen-at-Arms, 1993–
Colonel Sir Brian Barttelot, Bart OBE DL
Temporary Equerry to Her Majesty the Queen, 1970–1971
Member of Her Majesty's Body Guard the Honourable Corps of Gentlemen-at-Arms, 1993–
Colonel Sir Piers Bengough KCVO OBE DL
Member of Her Majesty's Body Guard the Honourable Corps of Gentlemen-at-Arms, 1981–
Her Majesty the Queen's Representative at Ascot, 1982
Lieutenant-Colonel John Dymoke MBE DL
The Honourable the Queen's Champion and Standard Bearer of England

6 THE ECCLESIASTICAL HOUSEHOLD 115

The Right Reverend John Bickersteth KCVO
Clerk of the Closet to Her Majesty the Queen, 1979–1989

The Reverend Canon Ian Hardaker
: *Chaplain to Her Majesty the Queen*
: *Clergy Appointments Adviser*

The Venerable Percival Ashford
: *Chaplain General of Prisons, 1981–1985*
: *Chaplain to Her Majesty the Queen*

Dr William Cole LVO FSA
: *Master of the Music of Her Majesty the Queen's Chapel of the Savoy, 1954–1994*
: *Master of the Music Emeritus of Her Majesty the Queen's Chapel of the Savoy*

7 LORD-LIEUTENANTS AND CUSTOS ROTULORUM 122

Commander the Right Honourable the Lord Cottesloe RN (ret.)
: *Her Majesty's Lord-Lieutenant of Buckinghamshire*

Lord Gisborough JP
: *Her Majesty's Lord-Lieutenant of Cleveland*

Captain C. A. Farquharson of Whitehouse JP
: *Her Majesty's Lord-Lieutenant of Aberdeenshire*

Henry Elwes JP
: *Her Majesty's Lord-Lieutenant of Gloucestershire*

General Sir David Fraser GCB OBE DL
: *ADC General to the Queen, 1977–1980*
: *Her Majesty's Vice-Lord-Lieutenant of Hampshire*

The Right Honourable Lord Rix CBE DL
: *Chairman of Mencap*
: *Her Majesty's Vice-Lord-Lieutenant of Greater London*

The Right Honourable Tom King CH MP
: *Secretary of State for Defence (1989–1992)*
: *Secretary of State for Northern Ireland (1985–1989)*

Introduction

For a chosen few, the words 'By Royal Command' have a special significance. These are the men and women who belong to the household of Her Majesty the Queen, or who perform some other direct service for the Monarch. Many books have already been written about the Royal Household, but these have rarely included the views of members of the household staff, because of the restraint of confidentiality that rests upon them. This book is different, though. Apart from the Foreword, written by Dame Barbara Cartland, this short introduction and some linking text, it is made up entirely of contributions by people who either work, or have worked, in the Royal Household or whose duties involve, or have involved, direct service to the Queen.

In order to compile this unique document I first approached Sir Kenneth Scott, Her Majesty's Deputy Private Secretary at the time, with an outline of my intention. He saw no possible objection to the project and thought it 'an excellent initiative'. With this endorsement, I set about contacting people in different areas of the protocol world. It was still a difficult undertaking, for, although Sir Kenneth could see no objection, there is an established code that household appointees should never discuss their role openly. A major breakthrough was achieved with the participation in the project of the Earl of Airlie, Her Majesty's Lord Chamberlain and the most senior member of the Royal Household. With his support, the project achieved wider credibility, and I was able to secure articles from representatives of many of the major areas of service to the Queen. The book that follows is therefore in effect written by those who have given such direct service and, although they choose their words carefully

Henry Buckton with the Princess Royal, President of the Save the Children Fund, during a visit to a centre for young people with multi-sensory impairment in Glastonbury, March 1993

(Photograph courtesy of Mid Somerset Series Newspapers)

and reveal no official secrets, they nevertheless give us a vivid insight into their world. Despite the unique nature of many of the contributors' appointments, I have tried to group their contributions into thematically arranged chapters, so as to give the book a logical progression.

Although the book is not directly about the Royal Family, the appointments held by the contributors have given them a close-up view of the Monarchy, and what they have to say helps to throw light on its position in our society and its value to the nation. For instance, Sir Roger du Boulay, who was Vice-Marshal of the Diplomatic Corps, shows us something of how the Queen has influenced foreign affairs and of the importance of her role within the Commonwealth of Nations. The Earl of Lichfield is one of a select group of people who has helped to promote the Queen's public image, which also includes her dressmaker, Sir Hardy Amies, and her jeweller, Andrew Grima. Lord Rix, the Chairman of Mencap, shows us the importance of royal patronage to a British charity.

As well as these, the book contains contributions from the holders of a diverse range of appointments, including a Master of the Royal Household, a Private Secretary to the Queen, a member of the Medical Household, a Commander of the Royal Yacht *Britannia*, a Superintendent of the Queen's Messengers, the Queen's Champion, the Constable of the Tower of London, the Lord Lyon King of Arms and the Queen's Remembrancer. Together with representatives of the Queen's chaplains and various of her body guards and the Lord-Lieutenants of various counties, they collectively throw light on the importance of the Royal Family and the pageantry surrounding it, which still today make Great Britain the envy of the world.

HENRY BUCKTON

1
Behind the Scenes: The Royal Household

On 31 January 1952, the then Princess Elizabeth and her husband the Duke of Edinburgh left England to begin a tour that was intended to take them as far as Australia and New Zealand – although, as it happened, the hand of destiny would disrupt their travels. As she boarded the BOAC Argonaut at London Airport, Princess Elizabeth – the heir to the throne – could already claim a successful record of representing her country abroad.

In December 1936, when she was only ten, King Edward VIII's abdication and the accession of his brother, her father, as King George VI transformed the young Elizabeth from a potential heir to the throne to the immediate heir: next in line to the most prestigious title in the world. Shortly after Christmas 1936 the family had moved into their new home, Buckingham Palace, and the young princess's life would never be the same again.

Before undertaking State Visits in her own capacity, Princess Elizabeth had understudied her father. In 1947 she had accompanied him on a State Visit to South Africa, performing several duties in her own right, including the opening of a new graving dock at East London, named in her honour. In May 1948, six months after her wedding at Westminster Abbey, she and her husband were invited to France on a State Visit, at the request of President Auriol. The Princess opened an exhibition depicting British life in Paris, visited Versailles and attended receptions at the British and Canadian embassies. The royal couple were a huge success, cheered with enthusiasm wherever they went. Further visits abroad followed, during which Princess Elizabeth continued to establish her own links with some of the great world leaders; a notable example was her visit to Rome in April 1950, when she was granted a private audience with Pope Pius XII in the Vatican.

By the early summer of 1951 King George was diagnosed as having a slight inflammation of one of his lungs. This prevented him from carrying out many of his public duties, and Princess Elizabeth began to appear more frequently in his place. On 28 May she opened the Glasgow Exhibition of Industrial Power, followed the next day by the Perth Festival of Art. By July the King's health had improved enough for him to take the family on a quiet summer holiday at Balmoral Castle, where his younger daughter Princess Margaret celebrated her twenty-first birthday – although restrictions imposed by the medical staff of the Royal Household meant that the guests at the celebrations were limited to as few as possible.

The King's health then degenerated, and on 23 September his surgeon, Mr C. Price Thomas, performed a successful lung resection operation at Buckingham Palace. A State Visit to Canada by Princess Elizabeth and the Duke of Edinburgh was delayed until the King was sufficiently recovered, but on 7 October, amid shadows of uncertainty, the royal couple set out on a five-week tour of the Dominion that was a resounding success. Before returning home they visited Washington at the request of President Truman, enchanting the American people (the President pronounced Elizabeth to be the fairytale princess of his childhood come to life).

When Princess Elizabeth and the Duke of Edinburgh boarded the Argonaut at London Airport on 31 January 1952, King George VI (accompanied by Queen Elizabeth, Princess Margaret and the Duke of Gloucester) came to wish them *bon voyage*: father and daughter would never see each other again. En route for Australia and New Zealand, the royal couple stopped to make the now famous tour of Kenya, and it was while they were there that the news of her father's death reached the new Queen on 6 February 1952. The modern history of Great Britain had begun.

The Monarch cannot be everywhere at once, and the Queen's success is furthered by an army of specially chosen lieutenants who support, assist and represent her in many areas of life and through whom her principles and philosophy are conveyed to the world at large. Her Royal Household embraces a wide range of staff – from her Lord Chamberlain and her Private Secretary, via chaplains and members of her ceremonial body guards, to footmen, clerks and porters. Most of the contributors to this book are members of the Royal Household.

In this first chapter, though, we shall be hearing from a few individuals more closely connected with Her Majesty's day-to-day affairs: people who rank among her most senior and confidential advisers and aides. These are some of the people who are responsible for her daily round – whom she meets, where she goes – and for keeping abreast of her commitments and ensuring the smooth running of the whole apparatus of the household.

Perhaps the most important of the officials who make up the personal and ceremonial world of the Monarch is the Lord Chamberlain. A chamberlain is an officer charged with the direction and management of the private apartments of a monarch or nobleman, and the Lord Chamberlain of the Household (not to be confused with the Lord Great Chamberlain of England, which is a hereditary title) has control of the six departments of the Royal Household. His role has always been exceedingly important, but it has changed over the centuries. He used to appoint the Queen's chaplains, physicians, surgeons and so on as well as the royal tradesmen. The companies of actors at the Royal Theatres were traditionally under his regulation, and he was also formerly the licenser of plays.

The best way to describe the present role of the Lord Chamberlain is to ask him directly. Today's Lord Chamberlain is David Coke Patrick Ogilvy, thirteenth Earl of Airlie. He is also Chancellor of the Royal Victorian Order and Lord-Lieutenant of Angus. A former Scots Guardsman, he is now a member of the Queen's body guard for Scotland, the Royal Company of Archers.

The Right Honourable the Earl of Airlie KT GCVO PC JP
Lord Chamberlain of Her Majesty's Household, 1984 –

The office of Lord Chamberlain is one of great antiquity and can be traced back to the reign of Edward II (1307–1327). The King's Chamberlain, as he was formerly known, was one of the Great Officers of the Household and an important political figure, often acting as the King's spokesman in Council and Parliament. Until 1924 the appointment was a political one, and the holder of the office changed with each change of government.

Today, he is the senior member of the Royal Household, which is made up of six departments: the offices of the Private Secretary, the Keeper of the Privy Purse, the Master of the Household, the Comptroller of the Lord Chamberlain's Office, the Crown Equerry and the Director of the Royal Collection. His role and function is to oversee the conduct and general business of the Royal Household and to be a source and focal point for important matters that have implications for the household as a whole. His role is non-executive, and the post is therefore part-time. His specific responsibilities are:

> to chair meetings of Heads of Departments (Lord Chamberlain's Committee);

> to be available for consultation with Heads of Department to discuss household matters;

> to oversee the structure and operations of the household as a whole to ensure, in particular, that the most appropriate structure is adopted, that communications and co-ordination between departments are effective and that centralized functions are established and common procedures and policies implemented as required;

> to be closely involved, from the initial stages, with all senior appointments, including discussing all proposals before any potential candidates, or ensuring parties who might assist with the identification of candidates are contacted;

> to undertake ceremonial duties as required.

So that the Lord Chamberlain can perform his role effectively, Heads of Department are required, on a timely basis, to report to him and keep him informed of all important matters affecting the administration and operation of the household as a whole. Each Head of Department has the right of direct access to the Queen but, wherever possible, should discuss with the Lord Chamberlain beforehand important (that is, other than day-to-day) matters concerning the household to be raised with Her Majesty; if this is not possible, the Head of Department should report to the Lord

Chamberlain subsequently. The Lord Chamberlain's role and function is sometimes described as akin to that of non-executive chairman of a group of companies – the Heads of Departments being the counterparts of managing directors of a group's component enterprises.

As the Earl of Airlie has explained, the Lord Chamberlain used to be a political figure, changing with each government. Nowadays the political wing of the Lord Chamberlain's Office is represented by the Vice-Chamberlain, whose function is to perform a series of tasks directly between Monarch and Parliament. Sir Sydney Chapman was Vice-Chamberlain of Her Majesty's Household from 1992 to 1995. His description of his duties illustrates vividly some of the ancient and unusual customs that still figure in the Royal Calendar.

Sir Sydney Chapman MP
Vice-Chamberlain of Her Majesty's Household, 1992 – 1995

For more than three years I had the honour to be the Vice-Chamberlain of Her Majesty's Household. This is a political appointment, traditionally held by a senior government whip; I had been appointed a minister in 1988 and became the Vice-Chamberlain after the 1992 General Election. In addition to my normal 'whipping' duties (if such duties can be regarded as normal) I had three specific responsibilities: acting as the Hostage when the Queen opened the new Sessions of Parliament; delivering Messages to and from Her Majesty; and writing to the Queen every day the House sat.

Acting as Hostage was an annual event. The tradition dates back to the mid-seventeenth century when King Charles I was executed. After that, monarchs were not very keen to come to Westminster, which at that time was the sleazy end of the city (has anything changed?) and, to ensure their safe return, insisted on a suitable parliamentary hostage. The tradition survives; Her Majesty cannot leave Buckingham Palace until the Vice-Chamberlain arrives, and he cannot go back to Westminster until after the safe return of the Monarch. Thrice I survived this ordeal, and (now it can be told) the hardest part was leaving Buck House after the Queen's return. I rather liked the place, as well as the hospitality.

Carrying Messages to Her Majesty was done very much on an ad hoc basis, but each occasion required a personal audience, usually in her private suite. There were certain fixed events, such as presenting an Address on the Gracious Speech opening each Session of Parliament, that involved the carrying of Messages, but there were many other occasions, too, most of which seemed to involve getting approval for Double Taxation Relief Orders. When I had these meetings with the Queen, I was required to seek her consent to the particular matter in hand, but business was quickly dispatched, and we then chatted about all sorts of things for quarter of an hour or so.

Without doubt, the most time-consuming duty was the daily letter – or Message as it is officially known – keeping Her Majesty informed of events in and around the House of Commons. Originally, this was the responsibility of the Prime Minister of the day, but during Queen Victoria's reign it fell upon the shoulders of the Vice-Chamberlain. What is written is entirely a matter between the Queen and her Vice-Chamberlain; no one else, save her Private Secretary, knows or reads what is written – not even the Prime Minister. Traditionally, the Message must be written by hand and in the third person, but the most demanding requirement of all is the 6 p.m. deadline. At that time, it is taken to the Palace, and Her Majesty reads the missive just before or after dinner.

What does the Message contain? Obviously, important events in the Commons will be included, but the Vice-Chamberlain often has to leave the Chamber during a major debate in order to write his piece before the deadline. More certainly, the primary purpose of the

Message is not to give a précis of what is said (this can be gleaned from the media or Hansard) but to relay the background to what is happening and the feeling among our legislators. The Vice-Chamberlain must bury his own political prejudices so as to give his Head of State all the information in an unbiased way. However, at least one 'Messenger' concluded that Her Majesty would want to be appraised of the gossip and intrigue in the corridors of power – and, when appropriate, in a light-hearted manner; he hopes the Queen, unlike her great-grandmother, was amused.

In a period of forty months, I wrote almost four hundred Messages. How long were they? They varied, but the daily diet was usually about 750 words, so I must have written 300,000 words in all. I reckon, with due immodesty, that I became one of the best-informed MPs about the House, although, as a government whip, I could not speak in the Chamber. The Messages would be a mine of information if ever I was to write my memoirs – but, alas, I am bound by the Official Secrets Act and cannot divulge a word of them!

As we have seen, one of the Heads of Department who reports to the Lord Chamberlain is the Master of the Royal Household. He (with his understudy, the Deputy Master) is central to all ceremonial entertainment at Buckingham Palace and is also involved in the Queen's visits abroad.

We shall see throughout this book that many office-holders in the Royal Household are men who have held senior rank in the armed forces and therefore have long been closely associated with the Monarchy. A case in point is Vice-Admiral Sir Peter Ashmore, Master of Her Majesty's Household from 1973 to 1986. He has also served as an equerry not only to Her Majesty Queen Elizabeth II but also her father King George VI.

Vice-Admiral Sir Peter Ashmore KCB KCVO DSC
Naval Equerry to King George VI, 1946 – 1948
Extra Equerry to Her Majesty the Queen, 1952 –
Master of Her Majesty's Household, 1973 – 1986

My initial first-hand experience of our Sovereign came at the age of fourteen, when as a Dartmouth cadet I attended the Silver Jubilee Review of King George V in 1935, on board HMS *Iron Duke*. Two years later I stood under Admiralty Arch as one of those lining the processional route during King George VI's coronation ceremonial and was thrilled and elated by the privilege. At the RNC Dartmouth the King's Dirk was awarded to the best cadet and the King's Medal to the top academic, and a member of the Royal Family visited the college at regular intervals.

In 1944, when I was serving in the cruiser HMS *Royalist* based at Scapa Flow, King George VI visited us (among many other units of the Home Fleet) before D-Day, and the spirits of the whole ship's company soared in a way that had to be experienced to be believed. I was therefore thrilled when the war ended and I returned from the Far East to be sent as Naval Equerry to the King from 1946 to 1948.

When I retired from the Navy in 1972 I was fortunate enough to become the Master of the Household to Her Majesty the Queen for the next thirteen years. I officiated at Buckingham Palace investitures and was privileged to hear the recipients of gallantry awards, from the Falklands or Northern Ireland, telling the Queen something of their experiences. I also travelled abroad with the Queen on her many overseas tours and visits in HMY *Britannia*.

Whether it was King George VI in South Africa in 1947 or the Queen in Papua New Guinea, Australia, the Caribbean or any other country of the Commonwealth, Their Majesties always made a special point of meeting ex-servicemen. Their loyalty and devotion to our Sovereign shone out. At Honiara there was the Solomon Islands coast-watcher who had been bayoneted almost to death for refusing to speak to his Japanese captors; in New Zealand there was Captain Upton, VC and Bar. If there was one scene that exemplified such loyalty and devotion it was the ex-servicemen's march-past before Her Majesty in the square at Ouistreham for the fortieth anniversary of the D-Day landings: their pride as they entered the small arena to *Britannia's* Royal Marine Band, their chests thrown out, a wonderful swing in their stride, the past forty years dropping magically from them. Such loyalty is an infectious and vital part of our make-up and outlook, and it has been a wonderful strength to our armed forces over the centuries.

Lieutenant-Colonel Sir Blair Stewart-Wilson was Deputy Master of the Household and Equerry to Her Majesty the Queen from 1976 to 1994 and has been an Extra Equerry since 1994; he was also an equerry to the late Duke of Gloucester. His other appointments have included Colonel of the Irish Guards, ADC to the Governor-General of New Zealand, and Defence, Military and Air Attaché at the British Embassy in Vienna. If Sir Peter Ashmore touched upon Her Majesty's role as an ambassador in foreign lands, Sir Blair shows us the Queen's effects at home and explains something of the lasting and binding impression that she can leave with diplomats when they eventually return home. However, to emphasize another recurring point, he begins with a quotation.

Lieutenant-Colonel Sir Blair Stewart-Wilson KCVO
Deputy Master of the Household and Equerry to Her Majesty the Queen, 1976 – 1994
Extra Equerry, 1994 –

Good company and good discourse are the very sinews of virtue.
                                                        Izaak Walton (1593–1683)

The company of characters who are interesting, fun to be with and makers of laughter comes high on the list of things that I most enjoy. Such people enhance one's life, and I have been fortunate to have worked for two — one long ago and one more recently.

In August 1957 the rather old and slow New Zealand Shipping Company liner *Rangitiki* left Tilbury Docks and slipped slowly down the Thames. Among her passengers were the Governor-General designate of New Zealand and his wife (the late Viscount and Viscountess Cobham), their eight children — a family of almost biblical proportions — and, among many others, myself as one of the two aides-de-camp. So began two very happy years of working for a wise and good man who was always fun to be with and good company.

As the Queen's Representative in New Zealand, the Governor-General wrote personal reports to the Sovereign in his neat, easily readable handwriting. I never saw them, of course, but I am certain that Her Majesty must have read them carefully, among the myriad reports from all over the world and other documents in her red boxes. I am sure that the Governor-General's reports would have told her just what she needed to know and that they would have been illuminated by shafts of light-hearted fun, like sunlight breaking through clouds. Lord Cobham was the sort of man who would do that; laughter was never far away.

Much later — nineteen years later in fact — I had the extraordinary privilege and good fortune to be selected to work for another person whom I soon found to be interesting, fun to be with and invariably good company. This was none other than the recipient of all those reports: the Queen.

To work for, and with, Her Majesty was not just a privilege, it was a revelation. The Queen has to listen to seemingly never-ending questions, in reply to which she has to give decisions and advice. Those whom journalists love to call her advisers themselves constantly seek advice from Her Majesty, which is invariably given with wisdom and clarity. But the Queen is also a good listener and consultation and advice flow both ways.

Much of Her Majesty's work involves meeting and conversing with people, and I have often heard it said that she possesses that most enviable of gifts, the ability to make the person she is with feel at ease and to converse in a relaxed way, almost as if two friends were meeting again, with plenty of time to talk and often to laugh. Discourse with the Queen can work magic too. I remember one foreign ambassador arriving at Buckingham Palace with his wife for their farewell audience. For ten minutes or so, before showing them into the Queen's Audience Room, I sat talking with them in the Empire Room – or, rather, I should say that I talked to the Ambassador, while his wife sat ashen-faced, unsmiling and unable to articulate much in English. After their audience with the Queen the Ambassador was much the same as he had been before, but his wife was transformed. As she emerged from the Audience Room she gave the Lady-in-Waiting and myself a lovely smile and chatted happily to us both in quite fluent English while we made our way back to the Grand Entrance. As we went down the Minister's Stairs I could almost have sworn that she was floating on air, with her feet not quite touching the steps!

There is always ceaseless work for the Queen as head of her family, as head of her own domestic households and office teams, as Head of the Commonwealth, as constitutional Head of State, as head of much else besides and as a highly respected world figure who has been at her post for longer than any other. Nevertheless it seems to me that kings and queens and princes tend to be remembered not so much for how hard they worked as for their characters and how they lived. The fact that kings and queens and princes work hard, sometimes perhaps too hard, is often either taken for granted and scarcely considered or is obscured by the apparent glitter and glamour, pomp and ceremony and the public routine.

Queen Elizabeth II works hard by anyone's standards, but for me that can never obscure her essential lightness of touch and the humour that shines through as often as the Queen can make it do so. Her Majesty is a very special character to work for, interesting, fun to be with and always good company. When the need to be serious allows, laughter is – in spite of everything – seldom far away.

The Master of the Household's department accounts for the main bulk of Royal Household staff, and he and his deputy oversee the general entertainment at all royal palaces: Buckingham Palace, Holyroodhouse and Windsor Castle. Under them an interesting cast of supporting players, many performing ancient and unusual court roles, plays its part in creating the overall impression that the Monarchy leaves on visiting Heads of State or ambassadors.

The next in the hierarchy after the Master of the Household is the Assistant Master of the Household (General), who takes charge of all the Queen's domestic arrangements. Under him and the Lady Clerk comes the Palace Steward, responsible for the arrangements at table and other functions, one of whose duties before a banquet is to check the table settings with a ruler to make sure that every piece of cutlery is in its correct position. The Page of the Chambers works closely with the Vice-Marshal of the Diplomatic Corps and handles all the preparatory work for investitures and ambassadorial audiences at Buckingham Palace.

This branch of the household also employs people such as Pages of the Backstairs, who are the Queen's personal pages within her private apartments; the Yeoman of the Royal Cellars, responsible for wine stocks at all royal palaces; the Assistant Yeoman of the Plate Pantry, in charge of the under-butlers; the Pages of the Presence, who see to the comfort of the attendants of visiting Heads of State; the Queen's Piper; luggage porters; and footmen, whose tasks include carrying in

Prince Philip's early-morning coffee tray and exercising the corgis. The more important members of the household staff have their own dining room, and the job of setting and clearing away their tables falls on the Assistant Yeoman of the Glass and China Pantry.

The Palace Foreman is responsible for maintaining the furnishings and fixtures of Buckingham Palace. Under his control is a small troop of craftsmen, appointed by the Lord Chamberlain, which includes upholsterers, cabinet-makers, gilders, locksmiths, carpet-planners, a french-polisher and the chief restorer of drawings. One particular function that helps to add colour and flair to the Palace is that of the Palace flower-arranger, who travels between the royal palaces making the arrangements for floral displays and the royal tables and looking after any established potted plants. Despite this busy schedule, the flower-arranger's is only a part-time appointment.

In the particularly important area of entertaining, food and wine, the Assistant Master of the Household (Food) organizes the royal shopping list, so to speak, and ensures that enough food is stocked to cater for the Royal Family, members of the household staff and guests. The daunting responsibility for preparing the food – there may be anything up to 600 guests at royal banquets – falls on the Royal Chef. He has a number of lesser chefs to help him, headed by the Senior Sous-Chef and the Pastry Sous-Chef, as well as cooks, apprentices and kitchen porters.

Close to the heart of everything that has been covered here is a group of individuals who are privy to information from all quarters: the Queen's Private Secretaries – who, in their own way and through their own channels, can give advice on a wide range of issues. A Private Secretary, as the title implies, holds one of the most confidential positions in the Royal Household. One of Her Majesty's current equerries is Sir Edward Ford. Sir Edward previously served King George VI as Assistant Private Secretary from 1946 and retained this position in Her Majesty's Household after her Coronation. He continued to serve as one of her three Private Secretaries until 1967. Sir Edward is also Secretary and Registrar of the Order of Merit and Secretary to the Pilgrim Trust. He was appointed tutor to King Farouk of Egypt in 1936. During the Second World War he served with the Grenadier Guards in France and Belgium and later in Tunisia and Italy, being mentioned in dispatches from both fronts.

Sir Edward Ford KCB KCVO ERD DL
Assistant Private Secretary to King George VI, 1946 – 1952
Assistant Private Secretary to Her Majesty the Queen, 1952 – 1967
Extra Equerry to Her Majesty the Queen, 1955 –

The Sovereign has three Private Secretaries: one principal and two assistants. The senior of the two assistants now bears the title of Deputy Private Secretary. Although there is no distinction between the duties of the three, the Principal Private Secretary (or 'the Private Secretary', as he is generally known) is the Sovereign's principal personal adviser. The appellation 'Private' is important, since the Sovereign, as a constitutional Monarch, is *formally* advised by her Prime Minister and Secretaries of State, who are her official Secretaries. Normal contact with her ministers is carried out by the Private Secretaries. They are also responsible for arranging her public engagements (as distinct from incoming State Visits and State functions, such as the State Opening of Parliament, which are arranged by the Lord Chamberlain) – except for social entertainments, which are in the hands of the Master of the Household.

The Private Secretaries are responsible for Her Majesty's general programme of visits, both in this country and abroad; they arrange her audiences, deal with her correspondence and act as intermediaries with government departments. Each day boxes arrive from different departments (containing, for example, Cabinet papers, telegrams from overseas diplomatic posts and submissions for appointments made in the name of the Crown), and these must be opened and their contents sorted and submitted to the Queen.

The Sovereign must never be out of touch with her government in the United Kingdom (nor indeed with the governments of Commonwealth countries of which she is Queen), so one of the Private Secretaries must always be available to her, whether she is in London, at Windsor, Sandringham or Balmoral, aboard *Britannia* or on a private visit. (Accordingly, any of them must be prepared to forgo, for example, Christmas at home to be in attendance on the Sovereign at Sandringham or Windsor.) While they are in such attendance, the Private Secretaries are treated as 'one of the family' and have meals with the Queen and take part in any recreational activities (for example, shooting) if the work allows.

Close contact is maintained with the Secretary to the Cabinet and the Principal Private Secretaries of the Prime Minister and other senior ministers and with the Appointments Secretary at No. 10 Downing Street. When the Prime Minister comes to the Palace for his weekly audience with the Queen, he normally brings with him his Private Secretary, who takes the opportunity of exchanging news and opinions with the Queen's Private Secretary, thus keeping the offices of each up to date.

A great deal of a Private Secretary's time is taken up with correspondence, and great care has to be taken not to show favouritism or prejudice in such correspondence, for it is written in the name of the Queen. Similarly, he is responsible for seeing that the Sovereign is furnished with a speech on suitable occasions, although this will normally have been prepared or revised by the appropriate Secretary of State.

An Extra Equerry is an honorific appointment and normally carries no obligations. However, the appointee could be called upon to be in attendance on Her Majesty if required.

All Royal Household employees have an obligation of confidentiality concerning their time working for the Queen and other members of the Royal Family, although certain appointments, such as that of a Private Secretary, require particular discretion. This is also true of members of the Medical Household.

Dr David Illingworth served in the Royal Navy during the Second World War, before being demobbed as a Surgeon-Lieutenant and spent four years in hospital medicine before being let loose on the general public. He was Surgeon Apothecary to Her Majesty's Household at the Palace of Holyroodhouse from 1970 to 1987. Dr Illingworth's particular area of service is, of course, an extremely delicate one, and we should not expect him to give details of his duties, but he has been able, within the limitations of confidentiality, to tell us something of his experiences.

Dr David Illingworth CVO
Surgeon Apothecary to Her Majesty's Household at the Palace of Holyroodhouse, 1970 – 1987

As the first National Health Service doctor to serve Her Majesty at Holyroodhouse, I regarded my appointment as Surgeon Apothecary as the ultimate achievement and honour. However, although I was vigilant and careful to institute preventive measures, I was seen by others in the Royal Household as 'humorously decorative', in the words of the unforgettable 'Chips' (Lord Maclean, Lord Chamberlain from 1971 to 1984).

My passionate desire to deliver the first baby ever born in the palace of Holyroodhouse remained unfulfilled for over sixteen years. None the less, it provoked much mirth and led to one magnificent episode in particular.

My home telephone rang as I changed for a Palace reception.

'You're in luck, doctor. We have a female guest in labour,' said an anonymous voice.

Holyrood was reached at the speed of light; I was going to make history!

When I got there I found my patient was a vagrant duck that had waddled in from the Queen's Park to reproduce. As the eggs appeared it seemed quite unappreciative of its wonderful obstetrical location and the spontaneous appearance of the Royal Apothecary!

As I fancifully imagined the future ducklings boasting of their royal birthplace, I realized I had suddenly been left alone with the patient. I thought I got a distant glimpse of Chips Maclean, however.

If my suspicions were correct I got my own back at the next reception, though.

Faced with a large and drunken guest, noisily determined to show the Queen his war wounds, I coaxed the unsteady man into my room. He collapsed on the couch.

'The Lord Chamberlain will review your case,' I promised, which pleased him.

I went to find Chips and took him back to my room. However, the patient, instead of falling asleep, had prepared for clinical examination, and he erupted into the corridor as we arrived. We froze in horror as the huge man staggered past us wearing only a string vest and socks!

'Must see the Queen!'

Luckily, the pursuit was confined to upstairs corridors, and after two circuits our quarry was cornered in a kitchen. Swaying near the window, he mouthed, 'Get me the Queen, or I jump!' Chips cleverly distracted him by asking to see the wounds, and I slipped round behind him, only to see the Duke of Edinburgh deep in conversation with the King of Sweden underneath the window.

The next move was obvious. As I injected the man with paraldehyde, Chips gasped, 'Maybe you *are* more than just decorative!'

'Have I broken my duck?' I replied.

The latter part of my thirty crowded years in medicine was immeasurably enhanced by serving the Sovereign. When Her Majesty was in residence at Holyroodhouse my feelings of privilege reached a peak. I felt very responsible (but never anxious), and inevitably I fell under the spell of her magnetism. At my first introduction I experienced a great surge of emotion, and I recall a fanciful thought that my whole professional life had been leading up to this one dramatic moment, when the radiant young woman talking to me was the Queen – the apotheosis of our nation's history.

Sadly but understandably, no one will ever know of the dedication and courage I witnessed during seventeen years as a medical member of the Royal Household in Scotland. A pity! Those years are full of memories in which medical duties were accompanied and enriched by humour and admiration.

These are just a few of the people who come under the jurisdiction of the Lord Chamberlain and who, collectively, help to make the Royal Household function. By so doing they (along with those in the other departments) help to underpin the role of the Queen at home and abroad – a role to which she brings a length and breadth of personal experience and knowledge unequalled in the world today.

2
By Appointment to Her Majesty the Queen

THE words 'By Appointment to Her Majesty Queen Elizabeth II', carried proudly upon stationery, denote a honour bestowed on the individuals concerned – membership of the Royal Warrant Holders Association. Quite often it also indicates intimate working relationships that give expression to Her Majesty's ideas in many areas of life, both public and private. Our next contributor illustrates this point perfectly.

Over the years jewellery has been used not only to enhance the Queen's own image but also as a token of good relations between Britain and other states. It was the Queen's own idea to present jewellery as personal gifts to Heads of State or their spouses during her official visits abroad. The task of designing and producing these gifts was entrusted to Andrew Grima, who over the past forty years has had a close and continuous connection with various members of the Royal Family.

Princess Margaret and Lord Snowdon, Prince Philip, Princess Anne, Her Majesty the Queen and the Queen Mother – have all asked him to design jewellery for them. Andrew Grima was made a Freeman of the City of London in 1964 and is a Liveryman of the Worshipful Company of Goldsmiths.

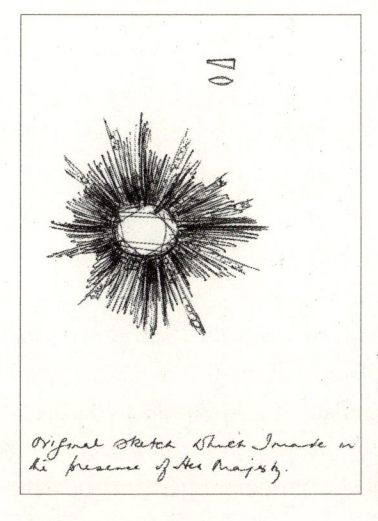

The original sketch made by Andrew Grima, in the presence of Her Majesty the Queen, for a brooch to present to Mme Pompidou during her State Visit to Paris in 1972

Andrew Grima
By Appointment to Her Majesty Queen Elizabeth II, Jeweller, 1966 – 1986

I entered the jewellery profession on demobilization in 1946, after spending nearly five years with the 7th Indian Division in Burma without being aware that the best rubies and some of the finest sapphires are found there. I have now been in the business for over fifty years, during which there has never been a dull moment. Without doubt, though, 1966 was the most exciting year in my career.

To begin with, my first shop – designed by my brothers Godfrey and George and incorporating sculptures by two Royal Academicians, Brian Neal and Geoffrey Clark – was under construction in Jermyn Street, directly behind Fortnum and Mason, and Lord Snowdon had agreed to do me the honour of opening it. Secondly, 1966 was the first year of the Queen's Award for Industry scheme. We entered, because we exported some 85% of our production and, of the 150 or so winners, received special attention because we were the smallest company among them. The excitement had hardly subsided when we heard that I had won the Duke of Edinburgh Prize for Elegant Design (the most prestigious design prize in the country, organized by the Council of Industrial Design) – the first time it had gone to someone designing individually hand-made pieces rather than industrial products.

The official announcement was made at a party on the top floor of New Zealand House, attended by the winners of the CoID design prizes, the panel of judges and Prince Philip, its chairman. The Prince asked me a great many questions about the pieces of jewellery in my winning collection. It was then that he decided to buy one of the items (a large brooch with carved rubies from an Indian headdress and gold and diamonds) for Her Majesty the Queen. It was this jewel that prompted the Queen to ask to see me at the Palace.

Some months later Lord Plunket, Deputy Master of the Household, telephoned to say that Her Majesty would like me to go to the Palace to discuss an idea that had come to her. (I remember wondering if I should take a taxi or drive into the Palace forecourt in my Aston Martin. I decided in favour of the latter – it was handmade, beautifully designed and British.) I was ushered into the Palace, and Lord Plunket appeared and took me up the stairs and into one of the reception rooms. Within two minutes he opened the door and stood aside to let Her Majesty in. She asked me to be seated and then expressed her pleasure in the ruby-and-diamond brooch Prince Philip had given her. She went on to explain that it had been the custom for the Royal Family, when making State Visits to the Commonwealth and travelling in Britannia, to present their hosts with Wedgwood dinner services; these were stored in crates in the yacht's hold. 'Now that we travel much more by air,' she said, 'it is very difficult to travel with all that china, so I had the idea that perhaps you would be kind enough to submit some designs for jewellery that would serve as a memento of our visit for our hosts.'

I worked feverishly at a collection of gold-and-diamond jewellery, all with the Royal Cipher in the centre, for our new and most important prospective customer. There were cuff-links for the men and three different types of brooch for the women, depending on the rank of the recipient. When all the designs were mounted in folders I telephoned Lord Plunket to tell him all was ready for Her Majesty to see, and within a week I was on my way back to Buckingham Palace. Her Majesty was very pleased with what I had produced and told me that in due course I would receive a letter from the Lord Chancellor's Office about the number of pieces needed.

After that our firm regularly made and supplied these gifts, as well as occasional 'special jewels' for very special people. Early in 1972 I was summoned to the Palace by Her Majesty to discuss a very special commission for a gift that she had to make during the coming months. I was ushered into the usual reception room and the Queen entered, accompanied by a secretary. She told me that she and Prince Philip were to make a State Visit to Paris, and she wanted something extra-special for Madame Pompidou. However, there was a difficulty. Relations between Britain and France had been strained for some time, and Her Majesty thought that it would be insensitive to present the French President's wife with a brooch that blazed the Queen's Cipher from its centre. I pulled a card from my pocket and quickly sketched a golden 'sunburst' brooch made of gold textured wire with, in the centre, a large topaz that would have its underside polished flat; this would permit the cipher to be seen only on close inspection by those invited to do so. Her Majesty thought it was a brilliant idea and told me to go ahead and design and paint two versions for her to choose from.

I executed the designs and sent them to the Palace. Some days later I attended an evening reception at Windsor Castle in honour of the Dutch Royal Family, who were visiting Britain. I joined the line of guests waiting to be greeted by the Queen and Prince Philip, and when I reached Her Majesty she whispered that she loved the designs and would I go ahead and make number one (the next morning I received a confirmatory note from Lord Plunket). Twenty years later, when I borrowed the 'Pompidou brooch' for my retrospective exhibition at the Goldsmiths' Hall, Madame Pompidou told me how much she loved it and asked me to be sure not to lose it!

There is no doubt that the Queen's small group of very skilful dressmakers has been of great assistance to her. Their efforts have ensured that Her Majesty has always conveyed the right image for the occasion, whether it be a State Visit, a banquet or a Royal Tour. Royal dressmakers may not themselves take part in State ceremony in the way that many other contributors to the book do, but when the Queen wears their creations, they help to represent her in a way that no other individual can do.

In the case of Norman Hartnell, one of her most famous dressmakers, his first great creation for the Queen was her wedding dress, made in 1947 when she was Princess Elizabeth. His masterpiece, however, was undoubtedly the Coronation dress itself. The Coronation of Her Majesty Queen Elizabeth II was one of the first royal ceremonies to be broadcast live on television, and Hartnell's fabulous dress was admired by millions (in fact Hartnell also had the daunting task of dressing the six Maids of Honour, Queen Mother, the Duchess of Kent, Princess Alexandra and the Ladies of the Bedchamber for the occasion). And for the very first formal photograph taken after her Accession the Queen wore a Hartnell décolleté dress of crinkled black taffeta. Each of his creations for her was an original admired by a captivated nation.

In 1951, when Princess Elizabeth and her husband set out for Canada on their State Visit, she wore creations designed by Hardy Amies. Between them Amies and Hartnell supplied garments for the royal wardrobe wherever the Queen went, and in this way helped to represent her throughout the Commonwealth and beyond. Decades later, the Savile Row studio of Sir Hardy Amies still supplies that special look for royal occasions. How did it all start?

Sir Hardy Amies KCVO
By Appointment To Her Majesty Queen Elizabeth II, Dressmaker, 1955 –

People often ask me how I became dressmaker to the Queen. The answer is that it was purely the result of having a good clientele. One of these clients was very grand: the Countess of Ellesmere. She brought her two daughters, the Lady Susan Egerton and the Lady Alice Egerton, to us to have their suits made. Lady Alice had recently become Lady-in-Waiting to Princess Elizabeth.

We were aware for some time that Princess Elizabeth had let it be known on several occasions how much she admired Lady Alice Egerton's clothes. Now her approval became official: she was soon to embark on the first tour since her marriage (in 1948) and wanted to order some clothes from us. Shortly after this we were notified that Princess Elizabeth was coming to see us at Savile Row. She was to be accompanied by Princess Margaret. The collection was shown privately in my office with only Betty Reeves and myself present. I remember the Princesses greeting us with smiles and handshakes, like any of the well-born English ladies on whom I had previously waited. Everything was relaxed but also totally business-like.

A few days later we were summoned to Clarence House. Sufficient warning had been given to allow us to prepare some sketches of the wardrobe we intended to submit. I already had a good idea of what kind of clothes I thought would be appropriate for a royal princess. I already had the idea that royalty should be dressed like royalty, so I used rich materials. I also wanted to get away from the cliché of the pale-blue dress; at the same time, blue was obviously going to be the Princess's great colour, dictated by those oversized blue eyes.

This first order consisted of two overcoats, two day dresses and two evening dresses. If this seems modest by modern standards, I can only say that at the time we were all immensely proud to have been asked at all. It was a new experience for us all, and none of us could have imagined then that it was but the prelude to forty years' service in designing clothes for Her Majesty the Queen.

A short time after the Princess's return from the Canadian tour, we were commanded to prepare another collection. This time it was for her forthcoming tour of Kenya and South Africa (which, in the event, was to be curtailed in Kenya by the death of King George VI). Once again Betty Reeves and I made several visits to Clarence House, first with sketches and then to supervise the fitting of the clothes. Looking back, I do not think the clothes in this collection were as successful as those we made for the Canadian tour. Because they were designed to wear in a hot climate they involved the use of thin materials, and it is more difficult to make regal clothes out of thin materials than thicker, richer ones. If a lack of experience was responsible in part for this collection being less successful, I am glad to say that we managed to correct the fault in subsequent lightweight designs for the Queen.

On our first visit to Buckingham Palace I was told that I could myself always use the Privy Purse entrance if I wanted, but that my staff should use the side entrance. When I go with sketches I make use of the privilege of the Privy Purse entrance, but if I have any bolts of material with me or, of course, if I am with any member of my staff, I go in through the side entrance with pride. We are shown up to our waiting room, which is a small room near the Queen's fitting-room. I think the latter was instituted by Queen Mary, and it is a large dressing-room with good light and space for the Queen to walk up and down to try the effect of a skirt in motion. I sit in the corridor outside the Queen's bedroom waiting to be called in after the Queen has been clothed by the fitter and the vendeuse.

Over the past forty years I have sat many times outside the Queen's door listening to the light murmur from within, interrupted quite often by the Queen's silvery laugh. Sometimes there is an ominous silence, but this does not always mean that there is trouble afoot; it is merely an indication of concentration. If it is a first fitting I may in spirit be concentrating also, but if it is a second or final fitting about which I have reason to be happy I have time to look around me.

In our first years of waiting on the Queen we were always anxious that Her Majesty should have exclusive designs only. In time we found this practice to be unfair, though, in that it deprived the Queen of the chance of wearing some of our most successful dresses. So now we often bring dresses from our collection to show her, and she appears to enjoy trying them on. We explain the good points of a particular dress which we intend to keep, show a sketch of the dress with the alterations proposed, and take with us bolts of materials which we intend to use and which will be used only for the Queen. In this way the Queen has the advantage of using a cut which has proved to be successful, but having it made up in a material that will not be seen on our other customers. Above all, I have felt from the beginning that the Queen needs clothes that help her in what I can only describe as her work (she once spoke of it to me as 'going about my business').

Her visit to Germany in 1965 had a great fascination for me, not least because the programme showed that the President of Germany was to give a banquet and reception in the Queen's honour at Schloss Brühl. The German State had already begun the painstaking process of restoring this extraordinarily lavish and elegantly decorated former summer palace of the Archbishop and Elector of Cologne to its former splendour. I knew the palace and its magnificent interiors, built around 1740, from earlier visits and from my two-and-a-half years spent on the Rhine as a young man, when I had visited the place often. What I remembered most about the building was the splendid stucco work and, above all, the beautiful blue-and-white tiles that decorate the summer dining-rooms and kitchens. Blue and white, I was soon to discover, were the official colours of the Archbishop Klemenz August and the Wittelsbach family. With these colours in mind, therefore, I submitted to the Queen suggestions for the dress to be worn and we were all delighted when she kindly accepted. We chose a pale-blue soft satin, in no way stiff, for the skirt. The bodice was embroidered in white beads and pearls in a rococo design which reflected the influence of the stucco decoration. My pleasure at the Queen's acceptance of our design was equalled only by the delight I felt when a card arrived inviting me to attend the reception; the excitement of seeing our Queen on that particular evening was intense.

The press very often shows a great deal of interest in the Queen's wardrobe on State Visits such as this. To accommodate this interest the Queen had given permission for sketches to be issued in advance, but with the express proviso that no sketch could appear before the Queen had worn the dress in question. Peter Hope Lumley, my public relations consultant, was with me, and he knew this as well as anyone, but his ingenuity came to the fore on this occasion. He had arranged with the artist Robb, who was on the staff of the *Daily Express,* to have a copy of our sketch of the Queen's dress sent over to his office as soon as we were certain that she was wearing it. This we were able to know from getting a glimpse of the Queen as she set off on the drive through Bonn to the banquet. Peter, who was there to see this for himself, telephoned Robb with the confirmation before he, I and my sister drove off to the reception, which was to be held after the dinner. The result of this careful planning was shown the next day in full glory on the front page of the *Daily Express.* Our sketch of the dress filled more than half the front page alongside a headline that read: 'The Queen Dazzles Them!'

The Queen is the perfect 'couture' customer. Clothes are ordered with the object of pleasing the audience, who are always enchanted. Unflattering photographs are ignored or laughed at.

I have been a very lucky man.

BY APPOINTMENT TO HER MAJESTY THE QUEEN

The Queen is one of the most-photographed Heads of State in the world. Photography has always been hugely important to the promotion of the image of public figures, particularly so in the case of the Queen, and a number of photographers have specialized in photographing her. In the early part of her reign there were names like Cecil Beaton, Baron and Karsh, but with changing times came changing attitudes in photography, and new photographers began to emerge, such as Peter Grugeon, Norman Parkinson and Tony Armstrong-Jones (Lord Snowdon), who married Princess Margaret in May 1960. In 1981 the photographer chosen to cover the most celebrated royal event since the Coronation – the wedding of His Royal Highness the Prince of Wales to Lady Diana Spencer in St Paul's Cathedral – was Patrick Lichfield (the Earl of Lichfield), a cousin of the Queen.

Lord Lichfield went from Sandhurst to serve in the Grenadier Guards from 1959 to 1962. However, when he began his photographic career in the 1960s being related to the Royal Family did not exactly help his cause, as he explains.

The Right Honourable the Earl of Lichfield
Royal Photographer

I decided that photography would be the career for me on the day I left the Army, 14 October 1962. I walked out of Wellington Barracks and I went to a studio (still in khaki), banged on the door and said, 'Can I have a job?'; they said, 'Three quid a week, and you can start tomorrow.' So I sold my car and got a push-bike and pedalled around London for three years. It was a big change from a Ferrari and the Officers' Mess at Chelsea to a push-bike pedalling around in the snow. My family didn't like the idea at all.

I've never felt that I am a member of the Royal Family – and in fact I am not. Technically, members of the Royal Family are related through the male line, and I am related through Queen Elizabeth the Queen Mother. I am not therefore counted in the line of heirs to the throne – although, of course, I have a certain connection through being a cousin. I had one advantage over other photographers in that I knew the Royal Family, but the disadvantage was that they could not be seen to favour me, so it took a long time to get my first royal commission. I was fairly well established in the fashion and portrait worlds before I got any royal commissions. The first one was to photograph the Duke and Duchess of Kent, on 17 March 1966. From there I graduated to doing various foreign royals, such as the Danish Royal Family.

There is also the question of whether a title helps you get started in photography. In the market-place it does not, because there is bound to be some animosity towards you, and, even if people hide their feelings, it is pretty evident sometimes that people just do not want to give you work. I remember going cap in hand to advertising agencies, trying to get work and very much disguising my name – to the point where the *Daily Mirror* once asked me to go and photograph Lord Lichfield. They knew I was called Patrick Lichfield, and they said, 'Go and photograph your namesake.' I said, 'He's terribly dull. I don't think he'll be at all interesting.'

When I started on the royal pictures, it was a fairly closed shop. Cecil Beaton was the Royal Photographer. (I once asked the Queen about an absolutely spectacular picture of her that he did in the year of her Coronation, with the sceptre, orb and crown and a wonderful background. She surprised me by revealing that the background – which I thought was Westminster Abbey – and the most brilliant bit of lighting was painted.) Tony Snowdon had done quite a lot, as had Baron before him, and various other sort of blurry, soft-focused social photographers from Bond Street. I didn't really want to shoot that way. I'd been trained on *Vogue*, so I knew my technique pretty well, but I thought one should photograph people more honestly, something that was very much favoured in the 1960s. Royal photography

Author Henry Buckton with the Earl of Lichfield at Lichfield Studios in Kensington

has changed dramatically during the time that I have been doing it, although not at all because of me. What happened was that a lot of different photographers got a look-in, Norman Parkinson being particularly successful, and there was no official Royal Photographer. I did get an official status when I did Prince Charles's wedding, but that was because they needed to appoint an official photographer for that occasion. Other than that, there wasn't really such a thing as a Royal Photographer, so we used to share and share alike.

Norman Parkinson once said that the Princess of Wales was the only member of the Royal Family best photographed in the street. Whether he meant she walks wonderfully well or she is photogenic in a paparazzi sense – which a lot of people are not – I agree that studio photographs of her have been less successful than the snaps people take. On the whole, though, I suppose all the Royal Family are easy to work with, so long as you are quick and know what you are going to do before you walk in. (I think a lot of photographers don't spend enough time on forethought – I suppose the Army taught me that time spent on reconnaissance is never wasted.) The other thing I do is to take copious test photographs before the real sitter arrives. In other words, if I'm photographing Prince Charles at eleven o'clock, I will probably have done lots of shots the day before of someone else in exactly the same pose, so I have it all worked out beforehand.

Some photographs are successful, others are not: there was a classically awful photograph of the Queen sitting in front of a one-bar electric fire. We do tend to get photographs that go wrong, and they always seem to happen on very important occasions. It has occurred to me that both the likelihood and the magnitude of a cock-up increase in proportion to the importance of the occasion: your tripod doesn't collapse when you're snapping your sister, but it does when you're photographing the Duke of Windsor.

I think royal photography has changed in that the technique has become very much quicker. This has allowed the technical quality of top photographs to get better. But if you look in detail at the early groups I did before I did the Prince of Wales's wedding, they seem somehow to lack a kind of cohesion; the photographer never appears to have been authoritative enough to get all the subjects looking at the camera at the same time. So, since in gatherings like these I have no such thing as authority, I invested in a whistle. I stood on my ladder and blew for all I was worth; they were so surprised that they all turned around, and I clicked.

Photography is a very recent invention, only one hundred and fifty years old. So the early pictures of Queen Victoria are very staid and studied. What contemporary photography has managed to do – particularly in the hands of Lord Snowdon, who was a great innovator – is to produce realistic pictures of the Royal Family, relaxed but not undignified. (It is a huge mistake to think you can take really relaxed pictures. You mustn't! The sitters must look dignified and relaxed but not casual.) I think it was Lord Snowdon who did some extraordinary pictures with Prince Charles and Princess Anne in the 1960s. After that, one began to see that some of the press photographs were getting really very good, and the sympathetic photographers were shooting really good pictures of them in the street. Of course, if you shoot enough film of anybody, something ought to be good. When one sees a news clip of Princess Diana walking into a film première, it's absolutely mind-blowing to work out from the amount of flash the amount of film that is exposed.

I think that in today's world the photographer's armoury has got to be fairly complete. You never know what you're going to be asked to do next, and sometimes you have to work under difficult circumstances. With the Royal Family you have be prepared to fit in with their schedules and where they are going to be. Having said that, one has to stress that they are the most phenomenally professional bunch of people. There's no point in asking them to do silly things, because they must stay dignified, but the setting can often relax the subject, and if I can I tend to do a lot of shots of them in the country. One group of pictures was taken while out riding at Balmoral. I'm not very keen on riding, but I had masses of cameras and no assistant, and I just went where the Queen went that day. I shot a hell of a lot, and all the pictures seemed to work. It was one of those gloriously lucky days.

Access to the Royal Family is not really that important. You obviously need to have access in order to get the pictures, but there is no point in taking off-guard pictures, because you know that they are not going to pass them. Everything has to be referred back and passed by the Royal Family or the Press Office. You can't just go up to Balmoral, shoot pictures and then come down to London and process and use them.

The royal wedding has to be one of the highlights of my career, and it was very flattering to get chosen for that occasion. I really was quite pleased with the photographs, and I suppose they brought me an international reputation. Although I had worked for *Vogue, Playboy, Life* and various other magazines in the United States, this was real international exposure. Interestingly, it was probably the last time that film of a big event like that had to be taken physically from London to New York or wherever. (Now it can just be sent down the wire.) When I came out of the royal wedding, with all my film in my pocket, to go round to the labs (probably the only place in London open on 29 July 1981) I was stopped by a man from American television.

'Look, I've got the cash, and you've got the stuff.'
'I'll never give you the film,' I said.
'I don't want the film. I want the Polaroid!' he replied.
I didn't let him have it!

Also in terms of the media, another area that can be extremely influential on the way the image of the Queen is projected to the public is the press and television. Whether she is on a State Visit or opening a factory in the north-east of England, the Queen's movements will be observed and documented by reporters, photographers and cameramen from both national and local papers or television. In recent years there has been a policy by some sections of the press to portray the Royal Family in a bad light, because that seems to sell more newspapers. However, it would take a very devious reporter indeed to find something bad to report about the Queen herself, who throughout her reign has represented all that is good about Britain.

In 1948, when the media was more courteous and discreet than it is today, the BBC decided to appoint a special reporter, responsible for covering royal events. The job was given to Godfrey Talbot, the man whom many people consider to have been the ultimate radio voice of the Second World War.

Between 1948 and 1969 he was the first official observer accredited to cover events at Buckingham Palace. Having joined the Corporation in 1937, he became a senior news reporter and commentator on the staff of the BBC from 1946 to 1969. His publications include *Speaking from the Desert* (1944), *Queen Elizabeth the Queen Mother* (1973), *Royal Heritage* (1977) *and Forty Years the Queen* (1992).

Godfrey Talbot LVO OBE
BBC Correspondent at Buckingham Palace, 1948 – 1969

I guess I may claim to have been 'On Her Majesty's Service' because I wore khaki through a world war and, mostly in our years of so-called peace, I beat a journalistic worker's path in and out of the Palace gates. In short, for all my professional life I have been one kind or another of what I call a 'licensed busybody'. The reference books, however, stamp me as 'broadcaster and author; a wordsmith'. Mostly, decade after decade, a staff man of the BBC: a war correspondent through Hitler's war; and then the Corporation's man, who was the first chap officially accredited to Buckingham Palace.

As a war correspondent I was made particularly aware of the Royal Family's connections with the armed forces. The links are not merely titular: the ranks and offices held by the royals are more than automatic chieftainships: they indicate knowledge and involvement. Full lists would be lengthy and tedious, but it is worth noting that, for example, Her Majesty the Queen is Lord High Admiral of the United Kingdom and Colonel-in-Chief of very many famous regiments. Her consort, Prince Philip the Duke of Edinburgh, is an Admiral of the Fleet, a Field Marshal and Marshal of the Royal Air Force. Queen Elizabeth the Queen Mother's record is of course long and lustrous – dare one say that the very special rank nearest her heart was Colonel-in-Chief of her Scottish family regiment, the Black Watch (Royal Highland Regiment)?

One of my own memories of my OHMS years comes from a day on the Italian front in early 1944. The Sovereign – it was, of course, King George VI then – came out to see soldiers who were fighting stubborn German divisions well north of Rome. I was already a seasoned war correspondent and I was presented to His Majesty. He shook my hand and looked me over, saying 'Now I see the Voice. The Queen and I have often listened to you – at Windsor, or wherever we were – speaking from El Alamein and the Western Desert in the BBC's nine-o'clock news bulletins.' He smiled and added, 'I think you've been our favourite broadcaster: you and Tommy Handley.' (I'd never before been bracketed with the star comedian of the ITMA shows!) He spoke also about his Consort back in the UK, worrying about him endlessly whilst he was away in war zones. He was of course referring to a Queen who was unparalleled in history, even at that time, and who in later widowhood was to be uniquely admired by the world for almost half a century as Queen Elizabeth the Queen Mother.

A later memory is of His Majesty's daughter (now Queen Elizabeth II), who spoke to me very personally about VE Day in 1945, when the war in Europe ended. As Princess Elizabeth, she watched the rejoicing crowds that night from Buckingham Palace. She described how she and her younger sister Margaret appeared on the famous balcony at least half a dozen times – almost every hour – standing and waving alongside her parents in response to the roaring and cheering crowds below. Then, she said, 'We were allowed to go down and join – incognito – the millions of people packed together, flag-waving and shouting . . . We had wanted to see what it was like looking up to the Palace balcony . . . We linked arms and were carried off our feet by the massed celebrators.' Her story went on: 'Very late, we once more stood outside Buckingham Palace and joined in the renewed shouts of "We want the King!" . . . We were successful in seeing my parents yet again . . . I think it was one of the most memorable nights of my life.'

3
Diplomacy at Home and Abroad

BRITAIN'S influence in the world has diminished as other countries have become more powerful. None the less, British influence is often subtle and sophisticated, touching distant lands in a way that other moral influences cannot do. The British Empire may now be a distant memory, but in many lands throughout the Commonwealth of Nations, British ideology, political values and philosophy – even eccentricity – are still cherished, long after British administration has left their shores.

This respect and admiration are not altogether what might have been expected. After all, many of the countries in question have reason, as a result of past colonial subjugation, to detest British values. That Britain remains influential and respected in countries where it might easily have been regarded with indignation is due to the relentless efforts of one person – Her Majesty the Queen, the finest and most successful ambassador Great Britain has ever possessed.

From 1960 to 1963 the Right Honourable Sir Peter Emery was Parliamentary Private Secretary in the Foreign Office – a position that made him well aware of the important part that the Queen plays in foreign relations. As a Member of Parliament, Sir Peter is one of that select body of people who serve the nation in its entirety – locally, nationally and internationally – and he believes that Britain is still a world power to be reckoned with and that the story of Queen Elizabeth II is the history of modern Britain.

The Right Honourable Sir Peter Emery MP
Parliamentary Private Secretary in the Foreign Office, 1960 – 1963

From her early days as a young girl in the ATS, serving with us all at war, to the wise and beloved Monarch she has now become – this record is the modern history of Great Britain. It is the life of Queen Elizabeth II. Our new Queen's face as she returned in sadness from Kenya, after the blow of her father's death had dragged her away from Treetops, made one realize that never again could she be the relaxed woman, without major cares of State, that she had been hitherto. Here, instead, was dedication to her country and her people – a dedication that is with her still.

Through the tenure of successive governments, and now ten Prime Ministers, her reign has seen tragedy, but also greatness; worry but also elation; and victories wrested out of defeat. That our Monarchy is not as relaxed and informal as those of Holland or Denmark is but a reflection of the nation that we are. Our Head of State is a world figure, respected even in many lands that have no ties whatsoever with Great Britain.

Today, too many seem to belittle Britain's role in the world, dreaming of the days of Empire, crying out for supposed glory and feeling that its sovereignty is limited by its membership of the European Union. But no nation is exempt from the international responsibility of co-operation for peace, of forgoing some of its autonomy in order to work more closely for the common good. The United Nations, the North Atlantic Treaty Organization, the European Union, and the Commonwealth are all fora in which Britain must play her part, and often forgo rights that she could have claimed in the past. Few, if any, Heads of State have so consistently represented their country's interests in all of them, and Queen Elizabeth II is held in respect in them all.

Our modern age may not offer the glittering vision of conquest and foreign adventure associated with the reign of the first Queen Elizabeth, but it is a time when, under our Monarch, Britain has adjusted to finding a realistic role in today's world. And it is in this world that our influence can still be felt and where Elizabeth II is envied and respected by so many nations.

The Queen pursues a relentless vocation of State Visits, tours and ceremonial duties. The attendance of a member of the Royal Family (and particularly that of the Queen herself) at any occasion – whether it be a full-blown State affair or a less celebrated charity event – adds a lustre, glamour, dignity and a cast-iron commitment that no other individual, not even a Prime Minister, can provide. It is partly because of this that British influence covers the world. Not all such events involve foreign travel, however. There is one place to which the whole world comes: London – where the most respected figure in the theatre of world diplomacy holds court. Here Her Majesty the Queen meets global representatives, very much on her own terms.

At the heart of London's grand world of ceremony and protocol is the Vice-Marshal of the Diplomatic Corps. Sir Roger du Boulay, Vice-Marshal between 1975 and 1982, was heavily involved with the organization of State Visits to this country and the entertainment of foreign ambassadors to the Court of St James. He was a pilot during the Second World War, after which his diplomatic career included service in Washington, New York, Lagos and Manila, culminating in appointments as Head of Chancery in Paris and Resident Commissioner in the New Hebrides. Sir Roger's narrative presents a political gallop through the 1970s. This wonderful decade for the

Monarchy and the nation as a whole was epitomized by Her Majesty's Silver Jubilee, celebrated in 1977 amid a euphoric national concord seldom seen since her Coronation (and echoed in 1995, during the celebrations of the fiftieth anniversaries of the end of the Second World War in Europe and the Far East). Sir Roger explains the role of the Diplomatic Corps' representatives in the capital and shows how the representatives of the world come together in London.

An ambassadorial role: Her Majesty the Queen and the Duke of Edinburgh are welcomed to the British Embassy in Rome by Sir Ronald and Lady Arculus during their State Visit in 1980

(Photograph courtesy of Sir Ronald Arculus)

Sir Roger du Boulay KCVO CMG
Vice-Marshal of the Diplomatic Corps, 1975 – 1982

The job of Her Majesty's Vice-Marshal is one of only two available to the Diplomatic Service that carry with them membership of the

Queen's Household. (The other is that of Assistant Marshal, who understudies the Vice-Marshal in all his work. Since anything I say about the latter goes for the former too, I shall not refer to the Assistant Marshal again in what follows.) As a household appointment the job of Vice-Marshal was not, in my time at least, much sought after, since 'serious' members of the service had their eyes fixed on other horizons and seemed largely unaware of the special contribution that the Monarchy makes to foreign affairs, let alone to our national life. Membership of the household was an unappreciated privilege.

When told that my next job was to be Vice-Marshal I was serving as British Resident Commissioner in the New Hebrides Condominium. As Head of Chancery in Paris, I had been at the heart of the State Visit by the Queen and Prince Philip to France in 1972, and two years later had organized their visit to the New Hebrides, but in all other respects I was totally unqualified for the job. However, my policy had always been to accept without demur the inscrutable will of the Foreign and Commonwealth Office's personnel department, and to go wherever that or the tide took me. I never regretted any of the jobs I was given, however outré, and I found myself enjoying that of Vice-Marshal above all.

As far as the FCO was concerned, I was no more than nominated for the post; the office might propose, but it was the Lord Chamberlain who disposed. The vetting by him, as Head of the Household, and Lord Michael Fitzalan-Howard, as Marshal of the Diplomatic Corps and my immediate prospective boss in the household, was far from the formality it was represented as being when I was told to report to St James's Palace. This interview gave me my first glimpse of what the job might entail: the extreme splendour of the surroundings, combined with the humour, informality and lightness of touch of the incumbents – provided you did your job and shared their dedication – at once set the tone. Evidently I did not drop too many clangers and, despite my complete and obvious cluelessness, I found myself accepted (more than accepted – welcomed) into a team serving what was and is far and away the most worthwhile institution in the country: the Monarchy.

The Vice-Marshal's job comes in two parts, household and governmental. Which of them most enthuses the incumbent depends on circumstances and inclination. Here I focus on the household side. For me this was unquestionably the more important, and I never had any doubt about where my priorities lay, even though the bulk of my time and effort was inevitably taken up by the government side.

On the household side of his job, the Vice-Marshal is deputy to the Marshal of the Diplomatic Corps. The Marshal and Vice-Marshal together look after all the Queen's dealings with representatives of foreign and Commonwealth governments accredited to the Court of St James (that is, to the Sovereign – who, for this purpose, is still deemed to hold court at St James's Palace). The Sovereign's dealings with diplomats are restricted to the ceremonial and social (under our constitution, Her Majesty does not do business with foreign governments or their representatives; her ministers and their officials do that on her behalf). However, the Sovereign formally receives those accredited to her on their arrival, entertains them from time to time and takes leave of them less ceremonially before they leave.

These ceremonial occasions are arranged by the Marshal, with the help of the Vice-Marshal. Despite the size of the Diplomatic Corps in London (some 150 Heads of Mission at the last count – who, with their staffs and families, make up a corps of many thousands), the Marshal's post is not a full-time job. It is seen as important, but not necessarily time-consuming: a job for a distinguished and retired senior officer of the armed forces, who can devote to it as much more than the necessary minimum time as his circumstances and inclination dictate. In my time Lord Michael Fitzalan-Howard and his wife worked very hard on the all-important welfare side of the job, giving practical expression to the Queen's wish that all accredited to her Court should feel at home and welcome.

As I shall describe later, the Vice-Marshal, has other jobs to do as well. However, to his role as deputy to the Marshal he is expected to bring knowledge and experience of the personalities and countries involved, familiarity with the diplomatic world and way of doing things and expertise in the fine points of protocol, as well as to stand in when the Marshal is ill or away. He holds the personal rank of Ambassador. As deputy to the Marshal, the main events of his year are the presentations of credentials by newly arrived Heads of Mission, the annual reception that the Queen gives for the Diplomatic Corps at Buckingham Palace and the State Opening of Parliament.

Since there are some 150 Heads of Mission of one kind or another in London, and an average tour lasts three years, it follows that every year about fifty Heads of Mission arrive and fifty leave. The Queen receives each one as soon as possible after arrival, and either takes leave of each one at a personal audience or (if the Head of Mission has to leave while she is out of London) sends the Marshal to do so formally. She receives Heads of Mission only when she is in London (some six or seven months of the year). She receives only one on any one day, because – even if it does not include any business – the presentation of credentials is a significant occasion that sets the tone of the mission and can have a profound effect on the state of British relations with the country concerned. If some fifty new Heads of Mission have to be received during the six months or so when the Queen is holding morning audiences in London, this means an average of two a week.

The audience is made memorable in many ways, including some that the unthinking mock. Though the event takes place at noon, the dress is full evening dress – with the option, where appropriate, of uniform or national dress – and decorations are to be worn in each case. The Queen sends the Marshal, in full-dress uniform (and the advantage of an ex-officer of the armed forces is that the uniform is very splendid) in one of her own carriages – the Town Coach, with two horses for an Ambassador, the State Landau with four for a High Commissioner – to the Head of Mission's Residence to escort him (or her) to the Palace. There the Vice-Marshal, in what is now full-dress diplomatic uniform (the old full-dress has been replaced by what used to be Levee Dress, but the gold lace and feathers are still lavish), has assembled the Embassy or High Commission staff. The Marshal presents the Head of Mission first. The Queen has the Permanent Under-Secretary of the FCO at her side but otherwise receives the Head of Mission alone for, first, the formal presentation, and then an informal talk. The latter then presents his staff, and finally the Head of Mission's spouse is presented. Afterwards the Marshal escorts the Head of Mission, and the Vice-Marshal escorts the staff, back to the Residence. There, with the formal part of the ceremony over, there is invariably a marked – and delighted – reaction, and a splendid champagne party often develops. The Marshal and the coachmen cannot stay long, because of the horses, but the Vice-Marshal often does.

It is easy to mock all this as wasteful flummery, but it is carefully thought through and frequently reviewed. For the Queen and the household there is an element of repetitiveness. But for the diplomat – however sophisticated, even blasé, he or she may be – the occasion is memorable. The carriage-drive through the heart of London is a unique experience, and the blend of splendour and informality never fails to catch the imagination. However the Head of Mission might have envisaged his mission before it started, as a result of the credentials ceremony it almost invariably undergoes a sea-change and a sea-change for the better. 'If that is what happens at the heart, it can't all be as bad as your press and television make out' – such was the constant refrain.

These ceremonies take place up to three times a week for six or seven months in the year, and – even after the business of climbing into uniform (kept at the office) and parading at Embassy and Palace has been reduced to a fine art – they still cut a considerable chunk out of the working day. Indeed, the essential qualification for a Vice-Marshal is not so much the ability to change from one elaborate outfit to the next in a few seconds flat (often four times a day or more), nor a bottomless capacity for alcohol (coupled with a knack of disposing of the surplus in the nearest plant pot), nor even the ability to remain standing for hours on end (the bobby's sway becomes habitual), but rather a faculty for concentrating doses of serious work into the all-too-brief interstices between these other agreeable diversions.

One of two annual milestones in the Marshal's calendar, and therefore also the Vice-Marshal's, is the Queen's annual evening reception for the Diplomatic Corps, held at Buckingham Palace every November. To this every Head of Mission is invited together with a limited number of staff members, including spouses: some 1,800 guests in all. It is deliberately made a very splendid occasion. All the State Rooms are brought into use. Dress is full evening dress with decorations (and tiaras for those who still have one, or can beg, borrow or steal one), but, again, uniform or national dress is an option for those who do not wish to involve Moss Bros. The Queen's policy on dress is to make the event stress-free without sacrificing the spectacle or sense of occasion. I found the Vice-Marshal's life at this time of year was beset with calls from those who claimed to 'hate dressing up' or to believe fine clothes 'undemocratic' and so asked if they could come in their ordinary working clothes. Over the years I developed my own formula for dealing with such queries, making it clear that the VIP could do as he (the complaints never came from women) liked, provided he did not mind looking foolish and discourteous. In point of fact, no one invited to one of these receptions need find it impossible to dress appropriately, and the vast majority of people thoroughly enjoy dressing up for the big occasion. And it was people like the Russians, with their prized uniforms, and the Ghanaians, with their incomparable kente cloths, who really came into their own in this reunion of the whole corps.

The missions are disposed round all the State Rooms for the start of the reception, with the Dean of the Corps (the senior Head of Mission) in the throne room, where the Queen emerges from the private wing, and the most junior (that is, recently arrived) grouped round the ballroom. The latter group almost invariably includes the Americans (who seem to change Ambassadors frequently), so that junior status by no means betokens insignificance. Indeed, one of the pleasures of diplomatic protocol is that importance and precedence do not go hand in hand. The longest-serving Head of Mission can, and frequently does, represent an otherwise quite inconsiderable country, and the important ones might have to take their place at the tail of the queue. But all have to be treated with perfect correctness in accordance with long-established rules, and by so doing many awkward choices can be (and are) resolved.

The spectacle, as the Queen emerges to the sound of a fanfare from her State Trumpeters and an expectant hush falls on the waiting throng, is magnificent. The Marshal escorts the Queen, the Vice-Marshal escorts the Duke of Edinburgh, and specially recruited members of the FCO escort the other members of the Royal Family; they stop and chat to each Head of Mission and as many other staff members as time allows. The Queen sets the pace, and one of the Vice-Marshal's duties is supposed to be to make sure Prince Philip does not drop too far behind. I soon gave up becoming (let alone looking) agitated as the gap yawned wider during the course of the round; I quickly learned that Prince Philip knew exactly what he was doing, whatever the appearances. While nothing would deflect him from having his say (often pungent and forthright), he would always catch up as the Queen neared the end of the round and was about to disappear back into the private wing.

There always seemed to be plenty to talk about; recent visits or special interests, like Prince Philip's in wildlife and the Princess Royal's in the Save the Children Fund, provided pegs on which to hang valuable, and for the recipients often memorable, exchanges.

The benefit generated by this direct contact between the Royal Family and the representatives of the whole world in London can hardly be exaggerated. It does something to counteract the ill-will and xenophobia generated by an irresponsible press.

When the royals have completed their round, which takes two hours or more, the ballroom and supper-rooms are cleared, and dancing goes on into the small hours. The Vice-Marshal's share in all this is minor; the Marshal and the Master of the Household bear the brunt. All the same, he is there, and it is a significant landmark on his horizon.

The bulk of the Vice-Marshal's time, however, is taken up with functions that he performs in his own right, rather than as deputy to the Marshal. The most demanding – and rewarding – of these stem from his position as the day-to-day channel of communication at working level between the FCO and the Palace on the whole gamut of foreign affairs and foreign policy. In practical terms this means, in the first place, co-ordinating the programme of overseas visits by the Queen and members of the Royal Family and inward visits to the Queen by overseas Heads of State.

In my time some fourteen members of the Royal Family were actively engaged in overseas visits, both official and 'private' (no visit by a member of the Royal Family can ever be completely private, least of all abroad). The Queen's programme was always top priority, but her overseas visits were relatively rare and always planned well in advance. Prince Philip's travels were much more multifarious. Queen Elizabeth the Queen Mother was then carrying out an active programme, and Prince Charles and Princess Anne were just embarking on their official overseas visiting when I began as Vice-Marshal.

It was obvious to me from the outset that the Queen and Prince Philip, with their unique experience and length of service, were major weapons in our armoury and needed to be carefully 'targeted'. However, over time the same became increasingly true of the other members of the Royal Family, and the concept of a co-ordinated programme became increasingly widely accepted in Whitehall during my time. The official 'Royal Visits Committee', of which the Vice-Marshal was the junior member, grew in stature and activity, supervising the development of a rational programme of inward and outward visits. This had to take into account not only the requirements of British overseas policy (including trade, where the Dukes of Kent and Gloucester played, and continue to play, such key roles) but also ministerial plans and private visits by members of the Royal Family – which could sometimes be in aid of some official purpose or tagged on to a worthwhile official engagement. With visits by fourteen royals to be co-ordinated, this was an area of considerable activity.

Scarcely less demanding was the Vice-Marshal's involvement with inward visits. Inward State Visits – that is, visits by an overseas Head of State as the personal guest of the Queen and Prince Philip – are organized by the Lord Chamberlain, but the Vice-Marshal is involved at all stages of planning and execution and works closely with the Comptroller of the Lord Chamberlain's Office. I was exceptionally fortunate in having the late Sir Eric Penn and, later, Sir John Johnston to work under and with. Both in their different ways were born impresarios and managed these superb affairs with unmatched flair and style, as well as meticulous attention to detail. A State Banquet at the Palace or Windsor is an unforgettable and incomparable experience.

After some twenty years of experimentation, the format was pretty well fixed by my time. State Visits are major set-pieces, so they cannot be too frequent (not least because of the disruption caused to Central London traffic). Three in a year was the outside limit, but two – in summer and autumn – was seen as preferable. The visits lasted from Tuesday morning (official arrival and State Dinner) to Friday morning (informal departure), with a number of obligatory functions in between (State Banquet, Guildhall reception and banquet, government luncheon and so on) and a number of options – usually including the inside of a day outside London, during which the visitor could pursue his or her particular interests. The visits normally took place in London but could be staged from Edinburgh or Windsor.

State Visits are scheduled two to three years ahead, and serious planning starts six months beforehand. As in all such matters, it is the detail that counts: play the wrong National Anthem (this has been done – although not in my time, thank goodness!) or forget to move the traffic islands in the centre of the Mall, and the whole effect can be ruined and the atmosphere spoiled. When it goes right, though, as it almost always does, State Visits are unbeatable adjuncts to foreign policy. Virtually ignored by the media (though less so now than twenty years ago), unless anything goes wrong, they constitute a crucial element in the execution of foreign policy. The mixture of splendid spectacle and heart-warming informality seldom fails to affect the visitors' attitudes (the next trick is constructive follow-up, but that is another issue).

I will give just two of the more controversial examples, out of many less controversial ones. The Queen's visit to France in 1972, and President Giscard d'Estaing's return visit in 1976, set the seal on our long-drawn-out negotiations to join the European Community; and the visit of President Ceaucescu of Romania was designed both to speed up the process of disintegration of the Eastern bloc and the Soviet empire and to bring negotiations for a beneficial trade agreement to a successful conclusion. The Romanian visit has been much deplored in retrospect – especially in the light of Ceaucescu's subsequent dictatorial excesses – and our adherence to Europe has been less than wholly successful or popular. None the less, at the time both visits achieved the aims they set out to achieve (and a bonus from the Romanian visit was the defection of Ceaucescu's secret police chief immediately afterwards).

State Visits only came rarely, however – and there were none at all in the Queen's Silver Jubilee year of 1977, when (Commonwealth tours apart) her time was entirely taken up in the British Isles. That year did, nevertheless, include a Commonwealth Heads-of-Government Meeting, a NATO Summit and a European Summit, all in London, not to mention the Jubilee Celebrations themselves, which were attended by a galaxy of Heads of Government. During that hectic summer the Vice-Marshal's household and government jobs became fused and virtually indistinguishable. One abiding memory is the first of those mass surges down the Mall to the Palace gates, with which we have become more familiar during recent celebrations of the fiftieth anniversary of the end of the Second World War. A second, on a smaller scale, is that of the Queen stopping to talk to a group of students during her walk from St Paul's to Guildhall and finding to her amazement that these eighteen-year-olds – brought up at the start of the revolutionary 1960s and currently studying at the London School of Economics – had thought it worth while to stay up all night so as to watch their Sovereign pass the next day. These two events brought home to many of us how deep and persistent was, and is, the fund of devotion to and respect for the Monarchy.

There were other blazing highlights, like Queen Elizabeth the Queen Mother's eightieth birthday and, more sombre but equally vivid, Lord Mountbatten's funeral. The latter provided an object lesson in the importance of meticulous attention to detail and thorough rehearsal – even though funerals, by their very nature, take place at short notice. When the enormous funeral cortège was rehearsed with skeleton units it was found, to everyone's surprise, that over the first few hundred yards of the slow march from Marlborough Gate to Westminster Abbey the first division of the Foot Guard had drawn well away from the gun-carriage, drawn by sailors. It was then realized that the Foot Guard's pace for the slow-march is thirty inches, while that of the sailors is eighteen. Rapid adjustments were needed to ensure that the escort still had the coffin in sight when they arrived at the Abbey.

Highlights apart, one of the Vice-Marshal's most important day-to-day functions was to make sure that the Palace received all the information the Queen might need about foreign policy – and that ministers were made aware of any reflections the Queen might have on the advice to be submitted. This was not just a matter of reportage of events; analysis and interpretation, also the background to developments and policy decisions, all came into it. Under our Constitution, ministers conduct business, but the Queen must be kept informed and has the duty of 'warning and encouraging' ministers. As part of the information process, the Palace is on the distribution list for all FCO telegrams, in and out, and gets copies of all dispatches. However, the greater part of the FCO's decision-making processes comprises more or less informal discussions, ephemeral minutes, letters, records and notes of hundreds of meetings; it was the Vice-Marshal's job to make sure the Palace was aware of everything it needed to know about this aspect and that it was aware of it in good time. To this end, he had to keep abreast of almost everything going on in the office, attend the Permanent Under-Secretary's 'morning prayers' when possible and get into or read about as many other meetings as feasible. So armed, he found himself several times a day on the telephone to one or other of the Queen's Private Secretaries to warn him of developments in the wind or fill in the background to decisions in the making.

Of course, the Vice-Marshal was not the Queen's only, or even major, source of information. Her Majesty saw both the Foreign and Commonwealth Secretary and his Permanent Under-Secretary fairly regularly, not to mention her weekly audiences for the Prime Minister. Her Majesty also received all Ambassadors and High Commissioners, and as Queen, in my time, of some seventeen realms other than the United Kingdom she was in frequent and regular correspondence with their Governors-General, which gave her access to sources of information and inside points of view not available to the FCO.

In short, the Queen was widely informed about foreign affairs and by 1977 had a length as well as breadth of experience no minister could match. Her function of 'warning and encouraging' was therefore not just an empty formula, and the Vice-Marshal found himself a channel not just for information to the Palace but also for a return flow of warning and encouragement, in the form of comment and query, reaching up to, but never exceeding, the limit of constitutional prerogative. This return flow was never brusque or overbearing, seldom even explicit. But to the alert official or minister a nod from that source was as good as a wink. A note from the Palace might record, for example, that 'The Queen was interested to read [such-and-such] and recalls that in 1953 Sir Winston Churchill commented [so-and-so]'. In such circumstances it would be a rash minister who did not at least take a second look at his ideas.

The Queen is bound to accept and act on advice formally submitted by ministers in the areas in which they are entitled to offer it. However, such advice seldom or never came cold to the Palace. It was almost invariably discussed informally before being submitted formally, and it frequently underwent a sea-change during that discussion process, although the origin of the change was often difficult to pinpoint. I will give just one example. In 1979 the question arose of whether the Queen would be well advised to go to Africa for the Commonwealth Heads-of-Government Meeting, due to be held in Lusaka. This caused much debate within Whitehall. There were worries about security as well as about embroilment in the controversial Rhodesian issue. As originally posed, the question was 'Should Her Majesty be advised to be present?' Put like that, it presented an insoluble problem: whose advice should prevail? The Queen, as Queen of some seventeen separate and quite independent countries, acts on the advice of seventeen separate and quite independent Prime Ministers. Normally their advice neither overlaps nor conflicts, but on such a sensitive Commonwealth issue how could conflicting advice be avoided? While this knotty problem was being informally chewed over, the original question somehow got turned round: it emerged that the Queen, as Head of the Commonwealth, was planning to be present unless any of her ministers advised her not to go. When it was put like that, none did. The Queen was present – and by her presence contributed significantly to the conference's historically beneficial results, as posterity will surely acknowledge.

This is just one example of how the Queen, without stepping one millimetre outside the boundaries of her constitutional role, can influence policy in quite significant ways and how the Queen's unique experience can be, and is, harnessed for the nation's good. It was a privilege to be a small cog in this process.

The themes of communication and the Commonwealth that Sir Roger has touched on here link with what he has said about the Queen's role in international affairs. They tie in, too, with what Sir Blair Stewart-Wilson has told us of his time as ADC to the Governor-General of New Zealand and how Lord Cobham kept Her Majesty informed about what was going on in his corner of the world.

What exactly is the Commonwealth? In 1962 it consisted of sixteen countries – all of which had previously been part of the British Empire – whose leaders met the Queen in London at regular intervals to discuss points of common interest. If British influence is declining in the world, then one would expect Commonwealth membership to have fallen by now to far fewer than sixteen; instead, the roll now stands at forty-nine (in 1996). This represents a billion people spread over every continent of the world, and – through the Queen's role as head of this vast fellowship – a quarter of the world's population is influenced in some degree by British philosophy and ethics. The Commonwealth is not necessarily a political, military, financial or even a social organization but a context in which States that share common concerns or interests can discuss and resolve them with fellow members who share in a common tradition. For many countries their membership is an important element of the international status that they have achieved.

The surprising thing is that many of the Commonwealth countries were often ruled with a heavy hand in the time of the Empire. Colonial attitudes were often bigoted and contemptuous, and the white ruling class often saw itself as superior to the native inhabitants of the countries that it ruled. None the less, since the decline of the British Empire and the achievement of independence by former colonies, more and more of them have looked towards the Commonwealth – through which, notwithstanding past adversities, they share a common historical background, a common political heritage, and a broadly common pattern of institutions. There are also countless other links between these nations, through sport, culture, commerce, industry and the professions. The Queen, as the Head of the Commonwealth, provides it with an important element of continuity that has a great deal to do with the organization's effectiveness.

Correspondence between Her Majesty the Queen and her Commonwealth Prime Ministers and members of the Diplomatic Corps – and that between the FCO in London and its foreign outposts – is not entrusted to the Post Office. Because its sensitivity requires an extra degree of security, a separate method of transmission is used. This is provided by the Corps of Queen's Messengers, or Silver Greyhounds, who travel the world inexhaustibly on the business of Her Majesty the Queen. In a career that began in 1946, as King's Messenger to King George VI, and ended in 1978 as Superintendent of the Queen's Messengers, Captain John Canning has probably covered more miles than any other Greyhound.

Captain John G. Canning OBE
Messenger to His Majesty King George VI, 1946 – 1952
Messenger to Her Majesty the Queen, 1952 – 1967
Superintendent of the Queen's Messengers, 1967 – 1978

After service in the Artists Rifles (now 21st Special Air Service) and the Royal Artillery, in 1946 I was appointed a King's Messenger (in the year of Her Majesty's accession the title changed to Queen's Messenger). After twenty-one years of global travel, I was appointed Superintendent of the Corps in 1967 and served in that capacity until my retirement in 1978.

One imagines that there have been Messengers, initially called Heralds, for as long as there have been Kings and Queens. Among early mentions of the existence of the corps is one from the reign of Henry VI (1470–1471) that refers to an emolument of fourpence-halfpenny a day! In 1662 the 'Forty Messengers of the Great Chamber in Ordinary', as the Messengers were then known, rode at the head of the wedding procession of King Charles II, and it is popularly believed that it is to him that the corps owes the attachment to its badge of the silver greyhound that has given its members their well-established sobriquet.

A Queen's Messenger is entitled to his badge after two years' probation. A badge is struck for every reign, after receiving the approval of the Sovereign. Each has the royal cipher at its centre, surrounded by the same motto as the Order of the Garter – 'Honi soit qui mal y pense' – with a ribbon of Garter blue. (There is, however, no connection whatever with the Noble Order of the Garter.) The corps has a complete collection of badges, going back to the reign of George I – every one, of course, bearing the added silver greyhound.

The history of the Corps has many epic references to the courage and resource of its members, who are entrusted with the carriage of any material too sensitive to be moved by other means. (Sadly, danger still, persisted during my service – during the course of which three Messengers were killed in air crashes and two suffered the trauma of hijacking.) Such material originates from the Palace, the government, the armed services, and – mostly and naturally – from the Foreign and Commonwealth Office. The corps has its office in the FCO's fine building in Whitehall, although the Messengers are not members of the Diplomatic Service: a rational and, as far as I was concerned, happy arrangement.

A Messenger's royal duties involve being an usher at the Queen's annual Reception for Heads and senior members of diplomatic missions accredited to the Court of St James and also going abroad to wherever Her Majesty might be, so as to carry out, or be ready to take back to London, messages of a sensitive nature. Travel on such occasions was especially memorable, for one saw the great admiration and affection in which Her Majesty is held abroad and saw the subjects of other nations accord her the same welcome that she always receives at home. Messengers are occasionally also called upon to go overseas when sallies are made by the Prime Minister or Foreign Secretary.

The routine work of a Messenger, however, is primarily concerned with carrying classified material to and from our diplomatic missions abroad. To carry out their duty with security the Messengers bear their own passport, in red covers embossed with the words 'Queen's Messenger' and carrying the words 'Charged with Dispatches' in the preamble inside. This entitles them to complete immunity for the material entrusted to their care; even X-ray examination is proscribed. On average, a Messenger travels some quarter of a million miles a year and spends more than half his time abroad.

In my day the corps numbered just over fifty. With the end of the Cold War, this has come down to just under thirty, but I hope the Silver Greyhounds may continue to run for many years yet.

From the Queen's Messengers carrying her correspondence around the globe, we move to the vessel that has so often

carried Her Majesty herself to distant lands on numerous State Visits. Britannia's former Commander, David Hart Dyke, explains that life on board had its moments of fun, as well as work.

Captain David Hart Dyke CBE LVO RN
Commander of the Royal Yacht, 1978 – 1980

After many years in destroyers and frigates, everything about the Royal Yacht seemed different. How refreshing it was to join an immaculately maintained ship with no armament and a superbly professional crew. The ship's company, a happy and finely tuned team, strove for perfection in their work of supporting many royal duties and State Visits – all of it carried out in the glare of the world's media, so there was plenty of scope for mistakes and adverse publicity. I well remember the pressures of straining to get everything right and the need to plan to the smallest detail when preparing for Royal Duty. But what fun we had, too, and how privileged we were to serve and work closely with many members of the Royal Family. The enjoyment of my time aboard was enhanced by working for a wonderful Flag Officer, Rear-Admiral Sir Hugh Janion, and I was very saddened by his death in 1994.

I felt that *Britannia*'s role was just as important as that of a man-of-war, at least in peacetime. It was evident to us all that, in projecting British interests all over the globe, the Royal Yacht was unique and the envy of the world. To observe at close quarters the impression that she made when visiting countries around the world and entertaining their Heads of State was unforgettable. In political goodwill achieved and trade agreements signed the importance of these visits to the nation was enormous, and in value-for-money terms *Britannia* seemed to be worth every penny.

My first taste of Royal Duty was a State Visit to Germany by the Queen. This was followed by State Visits to Saudi Arabia, the Gulf

States and Denmark. In between such events were the annual cruises off the west coast of Scotland after Cowes Week, a visit by the Queen to the Channel Islands, the installation of Queen Elizabeth the Queen Mother as Lord Warden of the Cinque Ports and a NATO exercise in the Mediterranean.

I was always struck by how much the Queen and her family enjoyed their holiday cruising around the Western Isles in *Britannia*. It seemed to be the Queen's only real holiday each year, away from official visitors. Lord Mountbatten was a regular visitor, and his death was a terrible shock to us all; I was honoured to be invited to his State funeral in Westminster Abbey and the memorial service later – both moving and awe-inspiring occasions.

I particularly enjoyed the Queen's visit to the Persian Gulf in 1979. We repeated the sequence of visits that I had made some ten years earlier, carrying the Political Resident, Sir William Luce. Before retiring as Britain's Ambassador to the Gulf he bade farewell to the various Gulf rulers and borrowed a frigate so as to do it in style. When I revisited the sheikhdoms in *Britannia* I found Sir William's name was still much in people's minds.

There were always nerve-wracking moments on Royal Duty but plenty of lighter moments as well. You might remember to send all the right equipment ashore for a barbecue, but if you forgot to include a box of matches for Prince Philip to light the fire with your whole career was on the line. On the other hand, on one occasion between State Visits during the Gulf trip, a small deserted island was chosen for the royal party to have a barbecue away from the public gaze.

All went well until two scruffy workers from an oil terminal appeared from nowhere and interrupted the royal cooking. They joined in unsuspectingly, and it was some time before they recognized the company they were keeping. Signed photographs of the Queen and Prince Philip were summoned up from *Britannia* and personally presented to the two amazed workers before they sped back to their work. I sometimes wonder what story they are telling today!

I am now one of many Commanders to have enjoyed a very happy and memorable two years on the Royal Yacht. Almost above all, I remember the magnificent receptions aboard, ending with a floodlit Beating the Retreat by the Royal Marine band. The Queen would be on the Royal Deck, surrounded by her guests and tapping her fingers on the guard-rail in time to the music, and tears would trickle down many distinguished faces. As soon as the guests had disembarked, *Britannia* would move away and sail majestically into the night, leaving an admiring gathering on the quayside waving to the end: another job well done. Indeed, this must be the refrain of the story of *Britannia*, and her crew, throughout a life that has brought great benefit to the country over more than forty years.

Having examined the main events in the diplomatic calendar, Vice-Marshal of the Diplomatic Corps Sir Roger du Boulay now outlines the rest of his duties – the bread-and-butter side – as well as the odd perk.

Sir Roger du Boulay KCVO CMG
Vice-Marshal of the Diplomatic Corps, 1975 – 1982

I might just mention one 'perk' that probably saved my life during my seven years in the job. I have long felt that, if part of any day is not spent on or with horses, it is a day lost. It was therefore an immeasurable boon when an introduction effected through the household gave me access to the Foot Guards' stables at Knightsbridge Barracks, where some dozen chargers were kept for London parades. They needed exercising, and so for all those years it was my life-saving privilege to ride for an hour or so in Hyde Park every morning and jolt my liver and lungs back to life after the exigencies of the day and night before. (It must be healthier, and is certainly more fun, to burn off the surplus rather than refrain from absorbing it.)

Those early morning rides; arriving at the barracks in the pre-dawn darkness to find the whole mounted regiment silently drawn up and waiting to move off, with nothing but the jingle of a bit or a subdued gleam from a cuirass to betray their presence; the occasional lavish breakfasts after the ride, too – all these are among my most pleasurable memories. Without the stimulus of such a start, how could one face day after day of over-eating and -drinking and interminable sedentary politeness?

The balance of the Vice-Marshal's job – the part which took up most of his time and energy – was that of Assistant Under-Secretary in the FCO responsible for, and in my time actively running, the Protocol and Conference Department. The protocol side was busy enough by itself. In addition to the Foreign Office, there had, in earlier years, been separate India, Colonial and Commonwealth Offices, each with its own ceremonial officer. By 1975 all had been amalgamated and the Vice-Marshal was doing all their jobs – and coping with a vastly inflated array of Ambassadors and High Commissioners as a result of the loss of the old Indian and Colonial Empires.

As Chief of Protocol, the Vice-Marshal's fate was to look after members of the Diplomatic Corps in London and administer their privileges and immunities as well as regulating their behaviour. Let me not be thought to contribute to the myth of cynical and out-of-hand diplomats trading on their immunity; they were for the most part admirably law abiding and responsible. There were, however, occasional lapses – on their part, but also on those of local police or authorities – and rectifying (or, preferably, anticipating and heading off) the lapses took up time. Moreover, new problems kept cropping up. For example, a spouse shares her legal partner's privileges and immunities; but should a live-in partner do so, as the Swedes tried to claim? The rules were devised for male Ambassadors with female spouses who kept house and did not 'work'; but, increasingly, both partners worked – and not infrequently it was the female partner who was the Ambassador. This sort of thing caused problems — by no means insoluble, but they took time to sort out.

The corps, one of the largest in the world, not only threw up an astonishing variety of problems, it also involved one in a murderous programme of entertainment: lunches and dinners nearly every day of the week and three or four receptions an evening. For the last it was essential to learn the back way out of every embassy and reception venue in the capital, so that one could arrive, make one's acte de presence, drift out (often within minutes, perhaps via the kitchen) and rush on to the next affair.

In this connection I might mention two other perks almost unique for a British diplomat in London. First, because the working day (including obligatory social functions) seldom finished before the diplomatic 'witching hour' of 11 p.m., it was considered essential that the Vice-Marshal had a flat in Central London; and for all those years I lived subsidized by the public purse, first just off Piccadilly and later in Ebury Street. It was part of the agreement with the Palace that the FCO provided this accommodation – other members of the household were provided with apartments in one or other of the London palaces. Secondly, a car and driver were made permanently available to the Vice-Marshal. This, it was said, was at the insistence of Prince Philip, who had observed one of my predecessors (royal eyes don't miss much), full of vodka, making his way out of the Russian Embassy to his battered Mini in pouring rain in order to fight his way through rush-hour traffic to his next reception and a subsequent dinner.

The conference side of the job had originally been a separate department. In 1945 the Foreign Secretary Ernest Bevin had to arrange the first session of the United Nations General Assembly in London at short notice. For this purpose he recruited en bloc Field Marshal Montgomery's 21st Army Group HQ movements staff, under its Brigadier. When the Brigadier retired, the Conference Department merged with the Protocol Department. Greatly to my good fortune however, two of the old staff officers were still serving in my time – both women of formidable competence and charm, who, having coped with Monty, had no hesitation in telling any Prime Minister (even Mrs Thatcher) with steely politeness what he or she could or could not do.

The Vice-Marshal's job was to co-ordinate all overseas visits by ministers, avoid clashes if possible (everyone wants to be seen in Washington when there's a new President) and ensure that the visits contributed to the prosecution of British policy overseas, rather than providing an agreeable escape from the English winter. He had also to fit inward visits by foreign Heads of State into the pattern of royal visits and supervise their detailed planning and execution. Such visits, more numerous and diverse than State Visits, required much more adaptability and improvisation, and here the former Army Staff Officers were an uncovenanted blessing. During my time security became a rapidly growing worry, and I was allowed, unusually, to recruit extra staff to cope with the new problems these worries imposed. I could rely implicitly on my experts in these fields and, although the Vice-Marshal had to carry the can for anything that went wrong, I was more often able to bask in plaudits that my staff had earned.

These and other jobs took up endless time and energy. I, for one, was never in any doubt that my priorities lay with royal matters, but it would distort the picture to give the impression that this was the only thing, or even the most time-consuming thing that occupied my working and waking hours. The government work was the bread and butter; the household work provided the icing on the cake.

I came into the household by chance. I certainly did not seek the job, was hardly aware that it existed and rather disliked what I knew about it before I was nominated. In the conventional FCO view, the job would normally have been a stepping-stone to a final Head-of-Mission post abroad, and I was in due course offered such an alternative. I had no hesitation in refusing, however; it came home to me with overwhelming force that scarcely any job within the gift of the FCO could offer greater variety, challenge, excitement, fun or reward (in all except the financial sense). I was sad to leave when I reached retiring age in 1982; I felt I was only beginning to get a proper grip.

Still, I went out with a bang. My term had been extended for a few days to allow me to play my part in the Sultan of Oman's State Visit, which we had been preparing for six months. My last day saw the explosion of the Falklands War and the shock resignation of the Foreign and Commonwealth Secretary, Lord Carrington, who marked his departure with an important champagne party in his office on my last evening. Having been to a memorial service for Lord Butler earlier, I made my appearance at the party in full mourning – morning coat, black waistcoat, black tie and so on. 'Ah! As always the Vice-Marshal is the only man properly dressed for the occasion!' was Lord Carrington's characteristic greeting as he met me at the door, and I plunged into what proved to be a memorable and typically light-hearted wake.

4
Ceremonies and Settings: History and Heritage

SEVERAL grand locations around the country are so closely associated with the Monarchy as to be almost synonymous with it. These are either royal residences or the settings for ceremonial in which they play an essential part. In this chapter we shall come across some of these settings, along with the orders of chivalry and the ceremonies involving the Queen that are associated with them.

It is the presence and persona of the Queen that are the essential ingredients in the success of State events, but the stage on which many of them are set, Buckingham Palace, adds to their magic. On this stage, she, above all the other elements, captivates the heart and imagination and remains the prima donna assoluta, unequalled and unrivalled by any national figure during her reign.

Buckingham Palace did not begin life as a royal residence but was built as the town house of John Sheffield, Duke of Buckingham, in 1703. At that time Windsor Castle was the main royal residence, and when in London the Monarch resided at St James's Palace. It was George III, distinctly dissatisfied with St James's, who sought a new London residence. He bought Buckingham House from the son of the last Duke in 1762, and since then it has been the home of all subsequent Monarchs (although Queen Victoria favoured Windsor Castle, feeling Buckingham Palace to be far too formal). The Palace has undergone considerable change during its association with the Royal Family, beginning in 1820 when John Nash was commissioned to design a new palace around the existing structure and ending in 1913 when Sir Aston Webb remodelled the East Front of the Palace in Portland stone. The eighteenth-century conception of the splendid interior of the palace, where Her Majesty entertains, has remained largely unaltered.

Buckingham Palace is also the Queen's point of departure for one of the major set pieces of royal ceremonial: the annual State Opening of Parliament. The British parliamentary system includes three distinct elements: the Monarch, who is the constitutional head of the Government, the House of Lords and the House of Commons. Until the reign of the first Hanoverian Monarch, George I (1714–1727), the Sovereign presided over Cabinet meetings and therefore had a direct influence on government affairs. This became impractical, because George I could not speak a word of English, and the First Lord of the Treasury, Robert Walpole, was appointed to chair the House – so becoming the first Prime Minister and effectively the most important and influential commoner in the land. If today the Queen does not have the same influence on policy that earlier Monarchs enjoyed, she has none the less remained the one figure who has constantly held office throughout the succession of governments during her reign. (The first time she formally opened the new parliamentary session was on 4 November 1953, when she delivered the first speech from the Throne to be made by a reigning Queen in the twentieth century.)

Parliament, in the modern sense, can be traced to 1265 when, under the direction of Simon de Montfort, representatives not only of the ruling class (in the form of bishops, barons and knights) but also of the people of each borough gathered together at the Royal Palace of Westminster. This palace complex, along with Westminster Abbey, dated back to the reign of Edward the Confessor (1042–1066). During the eleventh to fourteenth centuries it was extended, altered and rebuilt (often after fire damage), notably by William II (1087–1100), Henry III (1216–1272) and Richard II (1397–1399). The idea of splitting Parliament into two houses emerged in the fourteenth century, when the House of Commons began to meet in the Chapter House at Westminster Abbey, while the House of Lords remained in Westminster Palace. In 1834, however, the Palace of Westminster was almost entirely destroyed by fire, and the present Houses of Parliament (built on the same site between 1840 and 1888) housed both Lords and Commons under one roof – although in different chambers – and incorporated the magnificent Westminster Hall (the major surviving part of the original structure, built by William II and enlarged by Richard II) as a fine vestibule.

The procession from Buckingham Palace to the Palace of St Stephen, Westminster, for the State Opening of Parliament is watched by crowds that grow larger every year – and it is clear that they come from the four corners of the globe not to catch a glimpse of parliamentarians but to see the splendour of the Monarchy at its very best. Her Majesty, in the Irish State Coach, is accompanied by an escort from the Household Cavalry and is preceded by a separate coach, guarded by another troop of Household Cavalry carrying the Imperial State Crown. As Her Majesty reaches the Houses of Parliament, the air is filled with the sound of a forty-one-gun salute, and she is saluted at the Victoria Tower by the Captain of the Yeomen of the Guard and the Captain of the Honourable Corps of Gentlemen-at-Arms. She is then greeted by the chief Officers of State. A procession – including the Lord Steward, who walks backwards before her, and the Mistress of the Robes, who walks at the head of the Ladies-in-

Waiting – leads her to the Robing Room, where she puts on the same parliamentary robe that Queen Victoria wore on similar occasions. Preceded by the Sword of State, the Cap of Maintenance and the Crown, Her Majesty then passes through the Royal Gallery to the Parliament Chamber, where she takes her place on the throne, from which she reads her speech, setting out the government's policy for the new session.

Our next contributors show, however, that all this serious ceremonial also has its incongruities and lighter moments. As Vice-Marshal of the Diplomatic Corps, Sir Roger du Boulay was involved with the administration and arrangements for the State Opening of Parliament.

Sir Roger du Boulay KCVO CMG
Vice-Marshal of the Diplomatic Corps, 1975 – 1982

One other regular set piece in which the Vice-Marshal was closely involved was the State Opening of Parliament. The Marshal is responsible for mustering the whole Diplomatic Corps, plus the careful and always fraught selection of spouses – space for this function is at a premium – to attend this sparkling, wholly British and irrational occasion. (Irrational because the whole of the 'Establishment' – Executive, Judiciary and Lords spiritual as well as temporal – are present but only a handful of the people who really run the country – the members of the House of Commons and their leaders. These latter are summoned to appear when everyone else is assembled and only just manage to squeeze into the doorway.)

All except the people who really count – ministers and members of the House of Commons – are in full ceremonial rig: peers, bishops and judges, with their ladies in décolleté evening dress (with fur wraps if they are wise) and every diamond they can dig out from vault, bank or pawn-broker. The Ambassadorial Box is as close as anywhere to the throne, so one of the Vice-Marshal's perks is to find himself at the heart of this spectacle – even if it does sometimes mean being trampled on by the giant gold-spurred boots of the Master of the Horse, backing to make room for the Sovereign's entrance. On this occasion life is again unfair to women – men's uniform, apart from being flattering, is warm; the ladies, in their décolleté and tiaras, have to suffer but in a good cause: pour être belles.

As already explained, Her Majesty is welcomed on her arrival at the Palace of Westminster by the Captains of her two ceremonial body guards, the Yeomen of the Guard and the Honourable Corps of Gentlemen at Arms (both the captaincies are political appointments). Viscount Davidson, who previously served in both the Black Watch and the King's African Rifles, was Captain of the Yeomen of the Guard.

The Viscount Davidson
Captain of the Queen's Body Guard of the Yeomen of the Guard, 1986 – 1991

There are seven government whips in the House of Lords. The Chief Whip is also the Captain of the Honourable Corps of Gentlemen-at-Arms. The Deputy Chief Whip is the Captain of the Queen's Body Guard of the Yeomen of the Guard. The other five whips are also Lords/Baronesses in Waiting. When, therefore, a peer is appointed to the Whip's Office, he or she automatically becomes a member of the Royal Household.

I had the very great privilege of serving as Captain of the Queen's Body Guard of the Yeomen of the Guard for five years from 1986 to 1991. My first duty was to attend the military tailors to be fitted into the ceremonial uniform worn for the State Opening of Parliament and State Visits. Fortunately, my predecessor had a build roughly the same as mine. After a nip here and a tuck there, I was able to get into the black trousers with a gold stripe down the side

CEREMONIES AND SETTINGS: HISTORY AND HERITAGE

The Viscount Davidson inspecting the Yeomen of the Guard at St James's Palace

(Photograph courtesy of the Viscount Davidson)

(worn over black boots with spurs) and the scarlet coat decorated with gold epaulettes and lanyard. The whole outfit was finished off by a sword and a silver-topped stick and crowned with a Wellington hat with a plume of ostrich feathers.

At the State Opening of Parliament the two Captains, standing at the bottom of the stairs in the Victoria Tower, are the first people to salute Her Majesty when she steps out of her carriage. After she enters the Royal Gallery from the Robing Room, they join the procession through the Princes' Chamber into the Chamber of the House of Lords, carrying their hats under their left arm. When I first did this, one of my stepdaughters, watching the ceremony on television and seeing the ostrich feathers on the hat, rang her mother to ask why I was carrying a dead chicken on my arm!

One's duty to Her Majesty naturally takes precedence over other duties as a government whip, but it might be of interest to touch on some of these as well. It is one of the anomalies of our parliamentary system that government whips in the Commons (who, presumably, went there because they enjoyed speaking) are not allowed to speak, whereas those in the Lords (who do not necessarily enjoy speaking) have to answer debates and questions from the front bench on behalf of the government. The Deputy Chief Whip is spokesman for the government department that has no minister in the House of Lords – usually the one that has no Bill during that session. During my five years I was spokesman for Education, Transport and Energy and, before that, as Lord-in-Waiting was Whip (and thereby spokesman) for the Home Office and the Scottish Office. Politically, the most important duty was to persuade members of the House of Lords to support the government – but it would take far too long to describe how that duty is carried out.

I regard the five years when I had the privilege of serving Her Majesty as the most enjoyable and interesting period of my life.

Another of those who plays a part in the ceremony of the State Opening of Parliament is the Gentleman Usher to the Sword of State. Admiral Sir Desmond Dreyer, Principal Naval ADC to the Queen from 1965 to 1968, was appointed Gentleman Usher to the Sword of State in 1973 and remained in office until 1980, almost the same period that Sir Roger du Boulay was Vice-Marshal.

The Sword of State, for which Sir Desmond was responsible, is a large two-handed sword with a scabbard of crimson velvet that is decorated with eleven gold plates bearing royal emblems. One side of the guard is fashioned as a lion, the other as a unicorn. Sir Desmond also tells us about the Imperial State Crown and the Cap of Maintenance, which are escorted to Parliament by their own Ushers. Her Majesty's personal regalia includes two crowns: St Edward's Crown and the Imperial State Crown. St Edward's Crown is the official

Crown of England, with which a new Monarch is crowned, but it is the Imperial State Crown that is worn at the State Opening of Parliament (it is also worn at the end of the Coronation ceremony). The latter was specially made for the Coronation of Queen Victoria. Among the priceless jewels it contains is the Black Prince's ruby (actually a stunning spinel, given to the Black Prince by King Pedro of Castile in 1367 and worn by King Henry V in his crown-helmet at the Battle of Agincourt in 1415), the famous second Star of Africa diamond (part of the largest diamond ever found, the Cullinan Diamond, which was presented to King Edward VII by the government of Transvaal in 1907) and a sapphire taken from the Coronation ring of Edward the Confessor. Appropriately, the pearls mounted on the crown were taken from ear-rings that had belonged to the first Queen Elizabeth.

Sir Desmond's description of the Gentleman Usher's participation at the State Opening of Parliament makes us realize that protocol has its lighter side.

Admiral Sir Desmond Dreyer GCB CBE DSC
Gentleman Usher to the Sword of State, 1973 – 1980

As its name implies the Sword of State is only paraded on such State occasions as the Coronation and the annual State Opening of Parliament. On the latter occasion the Gentlemen Usher is responsible for its ceremonial conveyance from Buckingham Palace to the House of Lords. Three Gentlemen Ushers carry the Sword of State, the Imperial State Crown and the Cap of Maintenance in a State Coach escorted by a detachment of the Household Cavalry, leaving Buckingham Palace shortly before the Queen herself.

In the House of Lords a peer (invariably one who has held senior military rank) carries the sword before Her Majesty on her progress through the House of Lords to her throne, from which she delivers her address and then on her return to the Robing Room. After she has left to return to Buckingham Palace the Gentleman Usher again takes charge of the sword, and it returns to Buckingham Palace with the Crown and the Cap of Maintenance in the same State Coach, escorted as before by the Household Cavalry.

The first time I took part in this ceremonial I asked what I should do with the sword when I got back to Buckingham Palace. 'Oh,' I was told, 'you leave it on the billiard table.' The security arrangements were very adequate, but I could imagine the embarrassing headline if it was mislaid: 'Admiral Says He Left It on Billiard Table.' However, all was well, and on each occasion, when the ceremonial was completed, I and others were invited to have a glass of sherry with Her Majesty.

After Buckingham Palace, the place most closely associated with the Queen in the nation's mind is Windsor Castle. This is also the home of several aspects of pageantry, many of them involving a select group of gentlemen who have the honour of living within its ancient walls: the Military Knights of Windsor. Their present Governor is Major-General Peter Downward, who explains this privileged position. His military career from 1942 to 1978 – during which he served inter alia with the South Lancashire Regiment, the Parachute Regiment and the Glider Pilot Regiment – took in the Second World War, the Berlin Airlift, the Korean War and the Aden Emergency in 1966. He is also president of the British Korean Veterans' Association.

Major-General Peter Downward CB DSO DFC
Governor, the Military Knights of Windsor, 1989 –

The Military Knights of Windsor were formed by King Edward III in 1348 shortly after the Battle of Crecy. The foundation was created to assist English knights and landowners who, having been captured by the French, had been impoverished by paying heavy ransoms for their release; usually this meant selling off their entire estate and property. The members of the early foundation were known as Alms Knights, or Milites Pauperes, because of their dependence on charitable support, and until the nineteenth century they were nicknamed the 'Poor Knights'. Edward III provided these gallant warriors with accommodation in the Lower Ward of Windsor Castle.

In the same year he formed the Most Noble Order of the Garter, comprising twenty-six Garter Knights: the Sovereign, the Prince of Wales and twenty-four Companions. The Order also included the College of St George, of which the Alms Knights became part, as their successors still are today. The establishment of the Alms Knights was set at twenty-six, in line with the Garter Knights and remained the same until 1559, when, in accordance with the will of King Henry VIII, Queen Elizabeth I signed a statute creating a new establishment for thirteen Alms Knights, one of whom would be Governor. The latter was installed in the old chapel bell tower (which ceased to be the campanile in 1488, when the original chapel was replaced by the present St George's Chapel), now known as the Mary Tudor Tower. This has been the abode of successive Governors of Alms Knights/Military Knights ever since.

In 1833 King William IV changed the name of the Alms Knights to the more respectable title of the Military Knights of Windsor and at the same time introduced the uniform of Army officers on the Reserve. This is still worn today and comprises a scarlet tail-coat, sword, sash and cocked hat with plume. King Edward VII added the white cross-belt, with a breastplate bearing the badge of St George against the Star of the Order of the Garter.

The Military Knights of Windsor proudly claim to be the oldest military establishment in the Army List. The knights are all retired Army officers who, once installed, can expect to end their lives in the Castle. On installation, which must take place before the age of sixty-five, each takes an oath proclaiming his allegiance to the College of St George, together with his willingness to observe the Anglican faith as followed in St George's Chapel. He must also be prepared to undertake numerous duties over the year, most of which entail being on Church Parade every Sunday morning. Additionally, there are four Obituaries in the year, and occasionally a funeral or the laying-up of a Garter Knight's Banner. State Visits to Windsor Castle also require their presence, but for the Military Knights the main event of the year is the Garter Ceremony, when they lead the procession down the hill from the Upper Ward to St George's Chapel, the spiritual home of the Order of the Garter.

As Governor of the Military Knights I have a set period in office, and hopefully will make my third and last retirement from service in uniform at the end of the century. I can say without hesitation that it is a privilege to be associated with this ancient order, and, while we are all dependent on our Army pensions, the enjoyment and feeling of fulfilment more than makes up for any shortcomings.

Windsor Castle embraces one completely in its long and fascinating history, as does St George's Chapel (which, few people realize, is a separate entity, as a Royal Peculiar within the Castle itself). The Sovereigns who have lived here, many of them interred in St George's Chapel or Frogmore, have all left their mark in some way or another, and one is often acutely aware of their presence, both spiritually and materially. All of us Military Knights are fiercely proud of our history. The traditions and customs that have been handed down to us generate a strong urge to aim for perfection in performing our duties, particularly in the way of ceremonial. At times, this may prove more demanding on the less agile knights than on the newcomers. However, lessons learned over many years of military service (including the polishing of buttons) come to the fore, and personal pride and a sense of duty suppress the aches and pains of advancing years. The most satisfying part of our daily routine is to look up at the Round Tower and see the Union Flag flying proudly over the Castle. More uplifting still is to catch sight of the Royal Standard, indicating that Her Majesty is in residence, for then we know that we are on Her Majesty's service.

Windsor Castle has had a chequered history in terms of royal favour: much of its development was due to Edward III and George IV, who showed a particularly keen interest in it. The first castle at Windsor was erected by William the Conqueror after the Battle of Hastings in 1066, and it remains the oldest royal residence in regular use and the centre of British chivalry.

Synonymous with Windsor Castle, because of the Garter Service held there once a year, is the Most Noble Order of the Garter. For hundreds of years, membership of the order was confined to British or foreign royal families, or peers of the realm, a tradition that was broken when Sir Winston Churchill was appointed a Garter Knight. Every year Her Majesty the Queen and the Duke of Edinburgh lead their fellow Knights – each wearing a huge star that bears the red cross of St George encircled by the order's motto – in a splendid procession through the Castle to a Garter Service held in St George's Chapel.

St George's Chapel, Windsor, was built in 1240 by Henry III and renovated by Edward III when he founded the Order of the Garter; its rebuilding in the Gothic style on an adjacent site was initiated by Edward IV in the 1470s and completed in the early sixteenth century. As well as being the venue for the Garter service, it is here that many English Sovereigns lie at rest. Canon Alan Coldwells, a former Canon of St George's Chapel, Windsor, tells us something of the history of the Most Noble Order of the Garter and the traditions he inherited.

The Reverend Canon Alan Coldwells
Canon of St George's, Windsor, 1987 – 1995

King Edward III defeated the French at the battle of Crécy in 1346, as a result of the devastating effects of his longbowmen. He then laid siege to Calais, which surrendered the following year but escaped pillage and destruction through the pleading of his wife, Queen Philippa, and the bravery of the famous six burghers of the town. The story is told that, during the ball held to celebrate the event, the beautiful nineteen-year-old Joan, Countess of Salisbury, dropped her blue garter, to the ribald merriment of some courtiers. (Known as 'the Fair Maid of Kent', Joan subsequently married Edward, the 'Black Prince' of Wales, and by him became mother of Richard II.) The King, to save her profound embarrassment, is said to have picked up the garter and bound it below his left knee, with the words, 'Honi soit qui mal y pense' ('Shame on him who thinks evil of it'). Since the story naming Joan was first told long after the event, it is often thought to be invention, but the alternative explanations seem to be no more convincing.

Whatever its precise origin, Edward founded the Most Noble Order of the Garter, now the oldest Order of Chivalry in existence, in 1348. It was founded to fulfil the ideals of medieval chivalry, following on from a splendid feast and tournament of the Round Table (echoing King Arthur and his Knights of the Round Table) held four years earlier at Windsor. The order was to consist of the Sovereign, the Prince of Wales (appointed by the Sovereign, not of right) and twenty-four Knights Companions (perhaps two jousting teams of twelve a side). Its first magnificent feast was held in 1349 – the same year in which the plague (later called the Black Death) reached England. The order's spiritual home was to be the refurbished Castle chapel (dating from 1240), rededicated to Our Lady, St George and St Edward the Confessor.

In 1348 King Edward also created a new foundation, the College of St George in Windsor Castle, with the chapel as its centre of worship (its statutes date from 1352). The college was to be a self-governing community of priests, laymen and choristers dedicated to daily prayer for the Sovereign and all the faithful. In addition, Poor (now Military) Knights were appointed to pray daily for the Sovereign and his successors. In 1475 Edward IV commissioned the building of a new chapel; the result was the present magnificent building in the Perpendicular style, the final flowering of medieval Late Gothic architecture. The full title of the chapel is the Queen's [originally 'King's'] Free Chapel of St George. 'Free', that is, from the jurisdiction of any bishop or archbishop. From the outset the King wanted no outside interference in the affairs of the college or his chapel.

For some two hundred years an annual three-day festival of the order was held at Windsor Castle, and the Dean's present drawing-room was originally the chapter house where the members met to transact their business before a solemn act of worship. The festival slowly fell into decline and was finally abandoned during the nineteenth century. None the less, the order itself continued. Distinguished new members were appointed, including the 'Foreign' or 'Stranger' Knights, who are usually Sovereigns of other countries. Early in the twentieth century occasional celebrations were resumed, but it was not until 1948, the six-hundredth anniversary of the order, that King George VI revived the ancient Chapter Meeting, a procession through the Castle wards and a service in St George's Chapel. The Garter Day ceremony has taken place regularly ever since.

In St George's Chapel each Knight has a personal stall. Above the stall is a banner emblazoned with his arms, and on the pinnacle of the stall is a helm surmounted by a personal crest, mantling, and a half-drawn sword (symbolizing the defence of the Church). Sovereigns who are part of the order display a crown instead of a helm and crest. In addition, each Knight has an engraved and enamelled metal heraldic stall-plate. After a Knight has died all is removed except the stall-plate. From earliest days ladies were closely connected with the order (the first member of modern times being Queen Alexandra, wife of Edward VII), and they display a coronet (apart from the Queen, the Sovereign of the order). The first woman to be admitted as one of the twenty-four Companions was Lavinia, Duchess of Norfolk, in 1990. She was followed by Baroness Thatcher in 1995. Extravagantly ornate dress has been abandoned, but members of the order still ceremonially wear a hat and a blue mantle with the badge of the order on the left shoulder; a collar of red roses alternating with gold knots supporting a pendant of St George and the dragon. The stylized garter is worn below the left knee, but only with breeches; ladies wear their garter above the left elbow.

The College of St George now consists of a dean, four canons, two minor canons, a choir of sixteen to twenty boys and twelve men directed by the organist and choirmaster. There is a supporting staff, some with ancient titles such as the 'Virgir' and the 'Chapter Clerk'. The Military Knights of Windsor, who live within the Castle, parade in uniform during College Term and on ceremonial occasions, including Garter Day. The college also maintains a study centre, St George's House, founded in 1966, where courses and consultations for both clergy and lay people are held to examine issues facing contemporary society.

St George's choir sings evensong on most days of the week, and virtually all services are freely open to visitors. Some three hundred voluntary stewards help to care for those visiting the chapel on their tour round the Castle. Daily, for nearly 650 years, worship has been held in the chapel and prayers offered for the Sovereign, the Royal Family, the Most Noble Order of the Garter, the departed, the Church and the world. St George's is a noble place indeed.

We shall now turn from the Order of the Garter to Scotland's equivalent order, the Order of the Thistle and to Scottish heraldry. Our guide is Sir Malcolm Innes of Edingight, Lord Lyon King of Arms and Secretary of the Order of the Thistle. Sir Malcolm is also a member of the Queen's Body Guard for Scotland – the Royal Company of Archers – and President of the Heraldry Society of Scotland.

Sir Malcolm Innes of Edingight, the Lord Lyon King of Arms and Secretary of the Order of the Thistle, wearing the Royal Tabard

(Photograph copyright John Trushell and reproduced with permission)

Sir Malcolm Innes of Edingight KCVO WS
Lord Lyon King of Arms, 1981 –
Secretary of the Order of the Thistle, 1981 –

I was appointed Lord Lyon King of Arms in 1981. The Office of Lyon may be traced back to the pre-feudal Celtic High Seannachie to the Royal Line of Scotland, and at each Coronation, before any King of Scots could be crowned, Lyon recited the royal genealogy back to Fergus Mhor MacEarc, the progenitor of the Scottish Kings. The Lord Lyon is that

'King at Arms,
Whose hand the armorial truncheon held,
That feudal strife had often quell'd
When wildest its alarms'

(Sir Walter Scott, *Marmion*)

and it has been said that Lyon is the custodian of the spirit of Caledonia.

In relation to heraldry, my duties fall into two distinct aspects – administrative and judicial. I act administratively when granting new armorial bearings, this being an exercise of the Royal Armorial Prerogative assigned to Lyon by various Acts of Parliament. (Armorial bearings are constituted by beautifully illuminated letters patent prepared by herald painters, sealed with the official seal and signed by myself.) I act judicially when considering petitions regarding rights to armorial bearings that have already been established and recorded in the Public Register of All Arms and Bearings in Scotland (founded 1672).

Most of my judicial work is disposed of in my room or in chambers. This may be quite an informal procedure, and the justice administered in this context has been compared to the benevolent justice administered on the 'moot hill' of some old barony or thaneage, rather than the curt severity of the Magistrates' Courts. From time to time, however, I am called upon to hear parties in a contested case. Then I preside over Lyon Court (Scotland's court of chivalry), fully robed, and hear the arguments of the parties or their representatives, who may be an Officer of Arms (Herald or Pursuivant), an advocate (as a barrister is known in Scotland), or a solicitor. When I issue a judgement I must give out along with it an opinion setting forth why I have reached the decision given. Any judgement issued in Lyon Court may be appealed to the Court of Session (the supreme court in Scotland), and from that court to the Judicial Committee of the House of Lords (an appeal was taken from the Lyon Court to the House of Lords as recently as ten years ago). In the scientific system of Scots heraldry the simplest or undifferenced arms are those of the Chief of the Name or the Head of the Clan, and it is over such undifferenced arms that most litigation arises.

It is an offence in Scotland to use or display armorial bearings to which one is not entitled. Any one who does so may be prosecuted in Lyon Court at the instance of the Procurator Fiscal to the court. The Procurator Fiscal who investigates complaints gives offenders every opportunity to put matters right, and during my years as Lyon there have been only two prosecutions with subsequent fines. That is how it should be. The system of protection in relation to arms works well, and never before has so much authentic heraldry been used and displayed in Scotland.

The Lord Lyon King of Arms is, quite separately, Lyon King of Arms of the Order of the Thistle. By separate commission I am Secretary of that order and as such responsible for preparing the ceremonies of the order. The Order of the Thistle enjoys in Scotland a position similar to that enjoyed in England by the Order of the Garter. It may have been founded in the fifteenth century, but it was revived on 29 May 1687 by King James VII of Scotland and II of England. The installation of a new Knight of the Order takes place in the chapel of the order, a magnificent Gothic-Revival chapel designed by Sir Robert Lorimer, built adjacent to the south-east corner of St Giles's Cathedral in Edinburgh. At ceremonies of the Order the Queen wears a dark-green velvet mantle, a black velvet hat with white ostrich plumes and about her shoulders is the collar of the order formed of thistles, the plant badge of Scotland, and sprigs of rue (for the Picts). The most memorable services in which I have taken part were those in 1962 when King Olav V of Norway and the Earl of Home (later Sir Alec Douglas-Home, Prime Minister) were installed as Knights and in 1977, the occasion of the Silver Jubilee, when His Royal Highness Prince Charles, Duke of Rothesay (the title of the heir to the throne in Scotland) was installed.

Lyon is the Monarch's 'Supreme Officer of Honours in Scotland' and is responsible for the preparation and conduct of each of the State, royal and public ceremonials. When I appear on a ceremonial occasion, such as the opening of the General Assembly of the

Church of Scotland (Scotland's national Church) or the installation of a Governor of Edinburgh Castle, or make a Royal Proclamation, I wear the tabard that displays the Royal Arms as used officially in Scotland ('the ruddy lion ramping in his field of tressured gold' in the first and fourth quarters). The Royal Tabard is the Sovereign's most sacrosanct coat, and to strike or deforce Lyon in the Tabard has been held to be a treasonable act. When Lyon makes a proclamation wearing the tabard the voice of his proclamation is the voice of the Sovereign. Before each General Election the proclamation dissolving Parliament is made at the Mercat Cross in Edinburgh's High Street, which can be a very cold and draughty spot on an autumn or spring day, and the protection of the quilted tabard is much appreciated on such occasions.

A senior member of Edinburgh's financial community recently observed to me at a luncheon, 'I think you may have the most interesting job in Scotland.' I did not disagree with him!

Another place closely associated with the Royal Family is the Tower of London. Here, on the banks of the Thames, William the Conqueror built his original timber-and-earth castle. Since then the fortifications have grown and become a great deal more elaborate, and the history of the Tower has seen many changes. In its time it has been a royal palace and residence, a royal mint, menagerie, prison, arsenal and place of execution. Today it is best known as the home of the Crown Jewels, where the Imperial State Crown and Sword of State (mentioned earlier by Sir Desmond Dreyer) and other regalia are kept between royal ceremonies.

Some of the less terrifying aspects of the history of the Tower of London are described by its Constable, Field Marshal Sir John Stanier. Sir John was also the Queen's ADC General between 1981 and 1985.

Field Marshal Sir John Stanier GCB MBE DL
ADC General to Her Majesty the Queen, 1981 – 1985
Constable of Her Majesty's Tower of London, 1990 –

The Office of Constable of the Tower is one of the oldest in the land. The first Constable, Sir Geoffrey de Mandeville, was appointed by King William I in 1087. I am the 165th Constable in an almost unbroken line. My predecessors include some very remarkable figures. Not many people know that Archbishop Thomas à Becket was a Constable until his murder in Canterbury Cathedral – the only Constable to be both saint and martyr. Another strange choice for the job was Cardinal Ottobonus, who was the Papal Legate to the kingdom in the reign of King Henry III; he later returned to Rome and was elected Pope Adrian VI.

All the Constables except one have been appointed by their Sovereign (admittedly, some kings moved them on pretty quickly; during his long reign King Henry III appointed no fewer than thirty-two Constables). The single exception was Sir Thomas Fairfax, appointed by Parliament in the time of Oliver Cromwell. It would be nice to report that all had died peacefully in their beds, but this is far from the case. Many were imprisoned in their own Tower for displeasing the Monarch; some were beheaded and others killed in battle.

Happily, the place is more peaceful now, and the gravest danger is that of being bitten by a raven. Surprisingly, though, it is true to say that more people have been executed in the Tower in the twentieth century than any other. In other centuries, most of the prisoners were beheaded outside, on Tower Hill. During the two world wars, however, convicted spies were put to death by firing squad within the Tower. The last to die in this manner was executed in 1941, the same year in which the Tower held its last political prisoner: Rudolf Hess.

Many people ask me about my duties. They are not too demanding; I must be present to offer the Keys of the Tower to Her Majesty the Queen when she visits (so far, she has visited once in each of my six years as Constable). I am expected to welcome any other member of the Royal Family to the Tower and any foreign Head of State. In my time these last have included President Bush of the United States, President Mitterrand of France, Chancellor Kohl of Germany and His Majesty the Sultan of Brunei. Along with the duties, certain privileges attach to the appointment of Constable: every one of Her Majesty's ships that sails into the Pool of London under the guns of the Tower has to pay 'Constable's Dues' laid down by King Richard II. These consist of a barrel of rum for the Yeoman Warders and a bottle of port for the Constable. I am also entitled to take any sheep or cattle that fall off London Bridge. So far I have not had many, but, despite this, I still count myself very lucky!

Finally in this chapter, we shall look at ceremony and protocol in the world of the law. Sir Jack Jacob QC was the Queen's Remembrancer between 1975 and 1980 and Senior Master of the Supreme Court, Queen's Bench. The Queen's Remembrancer is perhaps the most diverse position we have looked at so far and is inevitably involved in the affairs of various other appointments.

Sir Jack Jacob QC
The Queen's Remembrancer and Senior Master of the Supreme Court, Queen's Bench, 1975 – 1980

The Office of the Queen's Remembrancer is one of the most ancient in the legal hierarchy. The first known holder of the office was appointed in the Exchequer of King Henry II in about 1154. His duties were 'to put the Lord Treasurer and the Barons of the Court of Exchequer in remembrance of such things as were to be called upon and dealt with for the benefit of the Crown'.

By the Queen's Remembrancer Act 1859, the then Senior Master of the Court of Exchequer was appointed to be the Queen's

Remembrancer. Under the J.A. 1873–1875 (replaced by J.A. 1925) the Senior Master of the Supreme Court was appointed to the office, and now the Lord Chancellor appoints the Senior Master of the Queen's Bench Division, who, by virtue of such appointment, holds the office of Queen's Remembrancer. On his appointment, the Queen's Remembrancer takes his oath of office before the Lord Chief Justice.

His responsibilities and duties are many, and some are colourful and ceremonial and involve State functions and occasions involving the Corporation of the City of London and the Goldsmiths' Company.

For example, the Queen's Remembrancer is responsible for preparing the list of people to be nominated for the offices of High Sheriff throughout England and Wales (except for the Sheriffs of the City of London and the High Sheriffs of Cornwall, Greater Manchester, Merseyside and Lancashire). On 12 November each year he attends a special court, presided over by the Lord Chief Justice (or, if he attends, the Chancellor of the Exchequer), to read out the names of all the nominees. The chosen people are approved by the court (which is, perhaps technically, a sub-committee of the Privy Council), and the names are entered in a roll. At a subsequent meeting of the Privy Council each name is 'pricked' with a bodkin by Her Majesty the Queen.

The Queen's Remembrancer also prepares the Warrants of Approval of Her Majesty the Queen for the appointment of the Aldermanic and Lay Sheriffs of the City of London. He has custody of the Great Seal of the Exchequer (newly made at the beginning of each Monarch's reign), and he witnesses its affixing to the warrants, signs them and, in recent years, personally presents them.

The Quit Rent Ceremony consists of the Corporation of the City of London, through its Comptroller and Solicitor, rendering to the Queen's Remembrancer on behalf of the Crown 'quit' (or token) rents for two plots of land. The first quit rent – two knives, one of which must be sharp and the other blunt – is for a plot of waste land called 'The Moors' near Bridgnorth in the County of Salop. This ceremony was first noticed in 1211, before Magna Carta, and is said to be the oldest surviving legal ceremony next to that of the Coronation itself. The second quit rent (according to Exchequer records first rendered in 1235) consists of six horseshoes and sixty-one nails in respect of a tenement known as 'The Forge' in the Parish of St Clement Dane in the County of Middlesex. A third part of the ceremony involves the outgoing Sheriffs of the City of London accounting for Crown revenues received by them – nowadays a nil return.

At the Trial of the Pyx a jury (composed of members of the Goldsmiths' Company) is empanelled to test and assay every year the new coinage minted by the Royal Mint. This proceeding was well established in 1281, in the reign of King Edward I, when a warrant was issued constituting a court for the Trial of the Pyx and commanding the Barons of the Exchequer to hold the assays 'in such manner as the King's Council was wont to do.' Since 1870 the trial has been held before the Queen's Remembrancer. It takes place in two parts: the first generally in February, when the Remembrancer attends to charge the jury, and the second is generally in May, when he attends again to receive their verdict and their hospitality at a lively luncheon.

Another ceremony is the swearing in of the Lord Mayor of London. The Queen's Remembrancer administers his Declaration of Office to the new Lord Mayor of London on the second Saturday of each November. This takes place after the traditional procession from the Mansion House to the Royal Courts of Justice, accompanied by many leading dignitaries of the City of London, when the Lord Mayor attends the Court of the Lord Chief Justice to be presented to the Queen's Bench Division by the Recorder of London. The document signed by the Lord Mayor remains in the Remembrancer's custody.

5
Guards and Body Guards

*H*ER Majesty the Queen, one of the best-guarded Heads of State in the world, has seven regiments of her own Household Troops, of which she is Colonel-in-Chief. These consist of five regiments of Foot Guards – the Grenadiers, Coldstream, Scots, Welsh and Irish Guards – and the Household Cavalry, made up of the Life Guards and the Horse Guards. The primary role of all these regiments is as front-line infantry and armoured units of the British Army. However, they also have a ceremonial role, in which, as their title implies, their function is to complement and serve the Royal Household. They form an integral part of, and add colour to, all major royal events, including the State Opening of Parliament, and there is no more splendid sight than a troop of the Household Cavalry – Life Guards in red tunics, Horse Guards in blue – sitting on black horses, with helmets and breastplates gleaming in the sunlight.

Another Army unit with a well-known ceremonial function is the King's Troop of the Royal Horse Artillery, a familiar sight at many royal occasions. It provides the gun salutes for the Queen's birthday, the State Opening of Parliament, State Visits by foreign leaders and other such events. General Sir Martin Farndale, who is Master Gunner of St James's Park, describes the links between the Crown and gunners throughout the Commonwealth.

Sir Martin Farndale KCB
Colonel Commandant, Royal Horse Artillery, 1988 –
Master Gunner St James's Park, 1988 –

The direct links between the Monarch and the artillery are long, reaching back to 1484, when Henry VII appointed the first 'Chief Gunner'. Since then generations of gunners served their Sovereign around the world, living up to their motto, 'Ubique', with greatest gallantry and distinction. In 1945 one in four soldiers of the British Army was a gunner, and in this century alone over 80,000 British artillerymen have been killed and thousands more wounded in action. On St Barbara's Day in 1950, His Majesty King George VI directed that he be known as 'Captain General' of the Royal Regiment of Artillery. In October 1947 he had already changed the name of the Riding Troop the Royal Horse Artillery to the King's Troop and Her Majesty graciously directed that these two titles were to remain unchanged during her reign.

On Remembrance Sunday, as her Majesty leads the nation in remembrance at the Cenotaph, and the guns of the King's Troop mark the event, Gunners gather at the Regiment's memorial on Hyde Park Corner, and wreaths are laid by Gunners from all over the Commonwealth. As Captain General, Her Majesty the Queen is the head of all gunners of the Commonwealth, serving or retired, and binds us together in her service and the service of our various countries. My duty, as Master Gunner St James's Park, is to keep her informed of our affairs, and we are deeply honoured that she takes such a close interest and on frequent occasions graces us with her presence.

In addition to her Household Troops, Her Majesty also has her own ceremonial body guards: in England, the Honourable Corps of Gentlemen-at-Arms and the Yeomen of the Guard; in Scotland, the Royal Company of Archers. The

Viscount Davidson has already mentioned the Yeomen of the Guard. Major Sir Fergus Matheson of Matheson, the Standard Bearer of Her Majesty's Body Guard the Honourable Corps of Gentlemen-at-Arms, now introduces us to this body of men, which, although the junior of the two English units, is considered to be Her Majesty's 'Nearest Guard'.

Major Sir Fergus Matheson of Matheson, Bart
Standard Bearer, Her Majesty's Body Guard the Honourable Corps of Gentlemen-at-Arms, 1993 –

In 1509 King Henry VIII, not content with a Yeomen escort, ordered the formation of a new and sumptuous Troop of Gentlemen to be known as Gentlemen Pensioners or Speres. 'The Kynge ordeined fiftie gentlemenne to be Speres, every of them to have an Archer, a demi-launce and a Castrel and every Spere to have three greate horses to bee attendaunte on his persone.' They took precedence as 'The Nearest Guard' over the Yeomen of the Guard, a body of fifty archers formed twenty-four years earlier by King Henry VII at his coronation.

The Band of Pensioners was essentially a mounted escort armed with spear or lance, designed to protect the Sovereign's person in battle or on progress around the country. Among their earlier exploits, they accompanied the King to France in 1513 and took part in the Battle of the Spurs. They attended their royal master at the Field of Cloth of Gold in 1520 and were conspicuous in competing with the French King's Noble Garde du Corps. In 1544 they accompanied the King overseas again and were at the siege of Boulogne, escorting His Majesty at his grand entrance, and in 1547 they were present at the battle of Pinkie against the Scots. In 1598, 'Queen Elizabeth went to Chapel on a Sunday, guarded on each side by Gentlemen Pensioners, fifty in number, with battle axes.' Only during the period of the Commonwealth, when Cromwell formed a body guard of forty gentlemen of his own choosing, has the Honourable Corps ever been suspended. At the Restoration, those Gentlemen Pensioners who had survived the Civil Wars marched on either side of King Charles II's coach with pistols in their hands. At the Coronation of King James II, they took part in the great procession, marching ten on either side of the King and ten also on either side of Queen Mary. In time, their role became a ceremonial one that, in one way or another, has continued through the succeeding centuries of loyal service to successive Sovereigns. In more recent times, members have readily rejoined the colours in time of trouble – as in the Second World War, when almost the entire Body Guard found active employment in uniform.

The title of Gentlemen-at-Arms was introduced by King William IV in 1834. Today, the Gentlemen are appointed by the Sovereign and are members of the Royal Household. To be eligible they must be retired officers of long and distinguished service, who have held a regular commission in a combatant corps of the British Army or Royal Marines and who were under the age of fifty-two on appointment. Retirement on reaching the age of seventy is automatic. The establishment is for five Officers, twenty-seven Gentlemen and the Axe Keeper and Butler, who is a senior retired Warrant Officer. The Captain is a political appointment and is always the Chief Whip of the House of Lords; the Lieutenant, the Standard Bearer, the Clerk of the Cheque and Adjutant and the Harbinger are promoted from among the Gentlemen. All Officers receive Sticks of Office from the Sovereign on appointment.

The Body Guard take part in most State ceremonies. At the funeral of King George VI, they were present at the Lying in State and marched on either side of the coffin in the funeral procession. They escorted Queen Elizabeth II into Westminster Abbey at her Coronation. Other duties include royal weddings, the State Opening of Parliament, the arrival of Heads of State at Buckingham Palace and Windsor Castle, the Garter Service at Windsor and services at Westminster Abbey and St Paul's Cathedral for the Orders of

Chivalry, if the Queen is present. Possibly the most spectacular occasion of all is the annual reception given by Her Majesty at Buckingham Palace for the Diplomatic Corps. The Gentlemen also always assist at the three annual garden parties that the Queen gives at Buckingham Palace.

The Standard in use today was presented by the Queen at St James's Palace in 1986, replacing one presented by King George VI in 1937. The uniform, basically that of a Heavy Dragoon Guards officer of the 1840s, is a red coatee with garter-blue velvet cuffs and facings, embroidered with the (Tudor) royal badge of the portcullis and worn with a gold pouch-belt of oak-leaf design and heavy gold epaulettes; the officers wear gold aiguillettes. The overalls are blue with a gold stripe, the helmet is gilt with white swan's-feather plumes and the gauntlets are white. Cavalry swords are worn and long ceremonial axes, well over three hundred years old, are carried by the Gentlemen.

Although the purpose of Her Majesty's Body Guard may have changed considerably over nearly five hundred years, we are still proud of our position as the Nearest Guard.

Major Sir Philip Pauncefort-Duncombe, who was appointed Harbinger of the Honourable Corps of Gentlemen-at-Arms in 1993, tells us about his role.

Major Sir Philip Pauncefort-Duncombe, Bart DL
Harbinger, Her Majesty's Body Guard the Honourable Corps of Gentlemen-at-Arms, 1993 –

The Honourable Corps was formed in 1509, but not until 1526 do records show the corps to have been fully officered, with a Captain, a Lieutenant, a Standard Bearer, a Clerk of the Cheque and Adjutant and a Harbinger.

The Harbinger's duties then were 'to provide quarters for the

Band of Gentlemen Pensioners when attending the King on a progress'. (The title of Gentlemen Pensioners was retained until 1834, when it was changed, by permission of King William IV, to the Honourable Corps of Gentlemen-at-Arms.) In 1865 the Office of Harbinger was abolished and the duties transferred to the Sub-Officer, one of the Gentlemen-at-Arms; the records do not explain this move. In 1927 King George V approved the revival of the ancient title of Harbinger.

The Harbinger receives an Ivory Stick from the Sovereign on appointment and wears aiguillettes. His duties include leading the Gentlemen to their posts on duty, assisting the Clerk of the Cheque and taking responsibility for running the mess in Engine Court, St James's Palace – which involves organizing the annual cocktail party, dinners and other social occasions.

How do the Gentlemen come to join the corps? Their appointment is not always due solely to having been a senior officer in the Army or Royal Marines; long before entering the corps they may already have had some sort of contact with the Queen. An example is Sir Brian Barttelot, who had been a Temporary Equerry to the Queen and Colonel of the Coldstream Guards.

Colonel Sir Brian Barttelot, Bart OBE DL

Temporary Equerry to Her Majesty the Queen, 1970 – 1971
Member of Her Majesty's Body Guard the Honourable Corps
   of Gentlemen-at-Arms, 1993 –

My first encounter with the Monarchy was at an investiture at Buckingham Palace. Aged six, I was granted the very special privilege of receiving from King George VI the medal of the Distinguished Service Order awarded to my father, who had been killed in Normandy while commanding the 6th Guards Tank Brigade in 1944. This made a very great impression on me, and from then on I was quite determined to follow my father's footsteps and join the Coldstream Guards.

I received the Queen's Commission in the Coldstream Guards in late 1961 and quickly became familiar with the precise art of Public Duties in London and Windsor. (I somehow avoided the traditional trap set by older subalterns, who told young officers on joining that they were entitled to shoot ducks in St James's Park!) In 1967, as Adjutant of the 1st Battalion, I first met Her Majesty the Queen when she came to visit us at Chelsea Barracks before her birthday parade that year. Three years later, while posted to Regimental Headquarters, I found myself appointed Temporary Equerry to Her Majesty, which involved standing in for the full-time Equerry at audiences and investitures at the Palace; fortunately I got on well with the Naval Equerry, Jock Slater, later to become First Sea Lord. I had the good fortune to meet a lot of most interesting people, and it was a very happy atmosphere to work in. I was under the supervision of Colonel Sir Eric Penn, the Comptroller of the Lord Chamberlain's Office, who masterminded all the ceremonial. He was a charming and immaculately turned out ex-Grenadier officer, though somewhat awe-inspiring. In response to his repeated requests of 'Do call me Eric', all I could ever manage was 'Sir'.

I was privileged to take command of the 1st Battalion Coldstream Guards in 1982. After an operational tour in Northern Ireland we returned to London for a spell of Public Duties, during which time the Queen did me the very great honour of coming to dine in the officer's Guard Room at St James's Palace for a reunion with former Coldstream Equerries. This was a unique occasion. The Queen's Guard regulations state that ladies may not dine – but who could deny Her Majesty dinner in her own Guard Room?

During my final tour of duty as a serving officer, running Headquarters Foot Guards at Wellington Barracks, I also carried out the duties of the Field Officer in Brigade Waiting, an ancient court appointment that involved responsibility for Guards of Honour at royal palaces, the Garter Procession at Windsor and attendance at the State Opening of Parliament, riding with Silver Stick (my opposite number in the Household Cavalry) in a carriage behind the Queen.

On retirement in 1992 I found myself almost immediately re-enlisted into Her Majesty's Body Guard of the Honourable Corps of Gentlemen-at-Arms, a splendid body of former Army and Royal Marine officers, formed in 1509, who provide the Queen's 'Nearest Guard'. We attend all State ceremonial occasions, wearing a magnificent heavy-dragoon-style uniform, and, in addition to providing what physical security we can with axes and sabres, we add a considerable measure of dignity and colour to these occasions. So long as I remain fit for duty, I understand that I can continue to serve Her Majesty in this way until I reach my seventieth birthday.

Colonel Sir Piers Bengough, as well as being a member of the Queen's Body Guard, is her representative at Royal Ascot. Commissioned in 1948, he finished his military career as Colonel, and subsequently Honorary Colonel, of the Royal Hussars (Prince of Wales's Own). As an amateur rider, his numerous achievements include winning the Grand Military Gold Cup on four separate occasions. Sir Piers, too, shows us how his other experiences led up to his appointment as a Gentleman-at-Arms.

Colonel Sir Piers Bengough KCVO OBE DL

Member of Her Majesty's Body Guard the Honourable Corps
  of Gentlemen-at-Arms, 1981 –
Her Majesty the Queen's Representative at Ascot, 1982 –

It has been my great privilege and good fortune to serve the Queen in three different spheres; in the Regular Army, as Her Majesty's Representative at Ascot and as a member of the Honourable Corps of Gentlemen-at-Arms.

Two days after leaving school towards the end of 1947 I walked into the London Recruiting Office and joined the Army as a private in the General Service Corps — the quickest way to achieve my ultimate ambition to join the 10th Royal Hussars (Prince of Wales's Own), whose motto was 'Ich Dien' ('I Serve'). This achieved, I arrived at Iserlohn in Germany as the proudest Second Lieutenant ever commissioned. Twenty-three years later I commanded the regiment into which the 10th and 11th Hussars had been amalgamated – the Royal Hussars (PWO) – and was further honoured in 1985 by being appointed its Honorary Colonel for a seven-year period.

Before retiring from the Army in 1972 I had the further good fortune to be invited to become a Trustee at Ascot – the royal racecourse – and I was privileged to become Her Majesty's Representative at Ascot in 1982. By an Act of Parliament (the Ascot Act of 1913) control of the racecourse was transferred from the Sovereign to three trustees of the Monarch's choosing – the senior being known as the Queen's Representative and responsible to Her Majesty – 'to use and employ the racecourse under the direction of Her Majesty for the purpose of the Ascot Races and so as to further and promote the welfare and prosperity of the Ascot Races'.

In 1981 I joined Her Majesty's Body Guard of the Honourable Corps of Gentlemen-at-Arms, the Sovereign's 'Nearest Guard'. This was instituted by King Henry VIII in 1509 as a new and sumptuous troop of gentlemen – composed of cadets of noble families and the higher order of gentry and originally called the Band of Gentlemen Pensioners – to be his personal body guard. Today it consists of five officers, as in earliest times, and twenty-seven Gentlemen all of whom except the Captain (a political appointment) have by rule to be retired officers of the Army or the Royal Marines and under the age of fifty-two when appointed.

All members of the corps are members of the Royal Household. Our duties are, in the main, to be on parade at State arrivals of foreign Heads of State, the Garter Service, the State Opening of

Parliament and at Her Majesty's diplomatic parties. In addition the corps is on duty when the Sovereign attends services of the Orders of Chivalry at Westminster Abbey and St Paul's Cathedral. At Her Majesty's garden parties members of the corps are also on duty, although not in uniform.

The Queen's Body Guard for Scotland, the Royal Company of Archers, was formed in 1676 by an Act of the Privy Council of Scotland. It carries out similar duties to the Gentlemen-at-Arms when Her Majesty visits her northern realm.

Another figure, who adds occasional colour to State ceremonies, particularly Coronations, is the Queen's Champion. The role of this hereditary title-holder, like that of Her Majesty's Body Guard, has become somewhat less aggressive and more ceremonial as the centuries have diluted the ability of barons, nobles and roundheads, to throw down the gauntlet. The thirty-fourth hereditary Queen's Champion is Lieutenant-Colonel John Dymoke, whose proudest moment must have come in 1953, when he carried the Union Standard at Westminster Abbey during Her Majesty's Coronation. After military service with the Royal Anglian Regiment, which took him to such places as India, Sumatra, Malaya and Aden, he became High Sheriff of Lincolnshire in 1979 and Vice-Lord-Lieutenant in 1991.

Lieutenant-Colonel John Dymoke MBE DL
The Honourable the Queen's Champion and Standard Bearer of England

My forebears have had the honour of being the Monarch's Champion – a hereditary title – since they came over from Normandy with William. Like those we served, we have had our ups and downs. The first down was when poor Sir Thomas Dymoke was beheaded on the

Lieutenant Colonel John Dymoke, with the Union Standard in Westminster Abbey, June 1953, at the Coronation of Her Majesty Queen Elizabeth II

(Photograph courtesy of John Dymoke)

direct orders of Edward IV, for reasons too complicated to discuss here. The King did, however, feel a little guilty and in due course heaped honours on Thomas's son, Sir Robert – who went on to do rather well, keeping his head firmly on his shoulders despite his acquaintance with Henry VIII and, more importantly, Katherine of Aragon.

I suppose it was inevitable that things should come a trifle unstuck during the Civil War, when the family was fined a huge sum of money 'for having a lewd and malicious title'. Notwithstanding this lurch into the red, the Dymoke of the day lavished several thousands of pounds (at 1650 prices) on the young Charles II. It took a few centuries to straighten the books, but all was not lost, for the Merry Monarch allowed us to put a couple of acorns and oak leaves in two portraits which we still look at in the dining-room. (Remember the oak tree after the battle of Worcester?)

The last time a Dymoke appeared in full armour and threw down the customary challenge was at George IV's Coronation in 1821. After that Prinny was a bit too lavish, and there were cutbacks in the coronations of his brother William IV and his niece Victoria. And anyway armour was slightly going out of fashion.

I had the honour of carrying the Union Standard in Westminster Abbey in June 1953. That was a memorable occasion. Everybody was, of course, in their glad rags (Moss Bros did a roaring trade), and the precision with which everybody performed was faultless – and so it should have been, as rehearsals had been personally conducted by the Duke of Norfolk, for whom I have everlasting esteem. But most dramatic and splendid of all was the majesty of our Queen. So radiant and so calm. Who wouldn't have given their life for her? Long may our Queen reign over us and my family continue to carry out their hereditary role for her successors.

6
The Ecclesiastical Household

*I*N 1521 Pope Leo X invested King Henry VIII with the title 'Defender of the Faith' for his championship of the Roman Catholic Church against the current of the Reformation that was gaining ground in other parts of Europe. Inevitably, though, the Protestant reforms that were sweeping through northern Europe eventually reached the shores of England. When the Pope refused to grant him a divorce from his first wife Katherine of Aragon, who had been unable to bear him a son, Henry took the opportunity to make a formal break from the Roman Catholic Church and declared himself Supreme Head of the Church of England. Today, the Monarchs of England still hold the title 'Defender of the Faith', but, ironically, the faith they defend is Protestant.

Her Majesty the Queen is titular Head of the Church of England, and all its clergy owe her their allegiance, but a select group of individuals have the particular honour of being 'Chaplains to the Queen'. In this chapter we shall hear from some of them, starting with the Right Reverend John Bickersteth, who was Clerk of the Closet from 1979 to 1989. The Clerk has the responsibility of being a channel of information, in particular concerning those to be appointed to the ecclesiastical household.

Bishop John Bickersteth

(Photograph courtesy of John Bickersteth)

The Right Reverend John Bickersteth KCVO
Clerk of the Closet to Her Majesty the Queen, 1979 – 1989

There is no head of the ecclesiastical household, since the Bishop of Winchester (Registrar of the Garter), the Bishop of London (Dean of the Chapels Royal) and the Clerk of the Closet rank *pari passu*.

'The Clerk of Closette kepith the stuf of the Closet. He preparith all things for the stuf of the aultrez to be redy, and takyng upp the trauers, leyyng the cuysshyns and carpettes.' So run the regulations set down for the household of King Edward IV in 1478. The earliest references to the King's or Queen's Closet are in an account for the years 1427–1429.

Five hundred and seventy years later the duties of the Clerk bring him much less close to the Sovereign than many of his predecessors were. In the early spring of 1660 the scholar priest John Earle, for example, stood proudly on English soil beside his restored King, after the long years of exile which he had shared with him, 'wandering from one debt-haunted corner of the continent to another'. His reward was to be made Dean of Westminster, whence he later became Bishop of Salisbury, 'a man of all the clergy', wrote one of his successors, 'for whom the King had the greatest esteem'.

Over the period that I was Clerk, I presented to the Queen for their homage nearly forty bishops and recommended two dozen or so priests to serve in Her Majesty's thirty-six-strong College of Chaplains. However, perhaps the most enduring among many memories of my ten years as Clerk of the Closet dates from 21 April 1986. The Dean of Windsor and I were entrusted by Her Majesty with the conduct of the Thanksgiving Service in commemoration of her sixtieth birthday, which was held in a packed St George's Chapel, Windsor. At the end I gave the blessing that the Sovereign had personally chosen. It comes from the Wedding Service in the Prayer Book:

> God the Father, God the Son, and God the Holy Spirit, bless, preserve and keep you; the Lord mercifully with his favour look upon you, and so fill you with all spiritual benediction and grace that you may so live in this life that in the world to come you may have life everlasting.

Amen to that, says Her Majesty's erstwhile Clerk. The nation is supremely fortunate to have such a person on the throne; long may she reign.

The Reverend Canon Ian Hardaker
Chaplain to Her Majesty the Queen
Clergy Appointments Adviser

The office of Chaplain to the Queen is as ancient as the conversion of the Anglo-Saxon kings to the Christian faith. The Monarchs' household chaplains ministered to their spiritual needs – and often also served as advisers and secretaries – saying Mass and singing the services for the King and his household. (For me, it is fortunate that today's chaplains have no singing responsibilities!)

Through the Norman and medieval periods the Chapel Royal – which always related to persons rather than to buildings – became more organized and larger. Up to the beginning of the twentieth century there were forty-eight Chaplains in Ordinary – each having, in lieu of wages, an annual allowance for court residence: a reminder of the days when they were required to reside at court on a rota system.

The present form of office was instituted in 1912, with the formation of a College of Chaplains consisting of the Clerk to the Closet (head of the college), a Deputy Clerk to the Closet and thirty-six Chaplains. The duty of each Chaplain to the Queen is to preach one sermon a year in the Chapel Royal at St James. On appointment a Chaplain to the Queen is, with his wife, presented to Her Majesty.

The Venerable Percival Ashford
Chaplain General of Prisons, 1981 – 1985
Chaplain to Her Majesty the Queen

The Church intercedes regularly for 'our Sovereign Lady Queen Elizabeth'. Sovereignty, we know, is the relationship between the supreme Head of State and those who are subject. But this vested power and authority, called sovereignty, comes not simply from accession to a throne or the adornment of a crown; it comes by a nation's response and esteem for what Her Majesty represents and, above all, for what she 'is'. The Roman Catholic theologian, Hans Kuhn, has said, 'Authority can no longer be allowed to rest on external title or office, but on an inner authority . . . based on personal quality, factual competence and partnership.' The country at this time is indeed fortunate to be led by a Sovereign who exemplifies all. The high regard in which the Queen is held is the envy of nations.

All who are Chaplains to Her Majesty the Queen are vital and visible testimony to the Church's upholding of the Crown. The scarlet cassocks of Chaplains at Palace garden parties witness, hopefully, not to the prominence of the Church but, rather, its privileged support and admiration of the Queen. The Chapel Royal, in which the Queen's Chaplains hold the oldest office of all, has long represented a special connection with the Monarchy, of which it is proud.

Historically, a Royal Chaplain was in constant attendance on the Sovereign, even in war. His duties are now less onerous, but they are offered with the same genuine commitment to Her Majesty and express the wider goodwill of the Church as it regularly prays to God to:

> endue her plenteously with heavenly gifts; grant her in health and wealth long to live; strengthen her that she may vanquish and overcome all her enemies; and, finally, after this life, she may attain everlasting joy and felicity . . .

In this life, however, gratitude is due to a truly beloved Monarch – for the stability she has sought to give to the affairs of both Church and State and for duties fulfilled with a dignity and grace that has characterized a long and distinguished reign. Through her life of service, marked by Christian standards emphasized by example, she gives character to the nation. Long may she reign over us.

Finally, Dr William Cole explains his position as the Master of the Music of the Queen's Chapel of the Savoy from 1954 to 1994. The Chapel of the Savoy in London is the home of the Royal Victorian Order, which was founded by Queen Victoria in 1896, the five classes of which are bestowed on the

Monarch's personal initiative and are generally awarded to members of the Royal Family and staff for personal service.

Dr William Cole LVO FSA
Master of the Music of Her Majesty the Queen's Chapel of the Savoy, 1954 – 1994
Master of the Music Emeritus of Her Majesty the Queen's Chapel of the Savoy

The Savoy Chapel is that of Her Majesty the Queen in right of her Duchy of Lancaster and therefore is a 'free' chapel, not falling under any ecclesiastical jurisdiction. Her Majesty the Queen is the Duke of Lancaster, and the National Anthem that is sung at every service begins 'God save our gracious Queen, Long live our noble Duke.'

Although the chapel stands on an area of land given by Henry III to Count Peter of Savoy, the present building is all that remains of the Hospital of the Savoy built by Henry VII in 1512. The late King George VI, at his Coronation, commanded that the chapel should be regarded by members of the Royal Victorian Order as their chapel. All the order services for which I often composed special music took place at the chapel but, because it can hold only about 150, Her Majesty recently decided that the services should be held at St George's Chapel, Windsor, and the two choirs combine to sing the service. At the last service about a thousand members of the order were present.

The statutory service is on Sunday morning, but there are also many special services, weddings and memorial services. The chapel is noted for its music, and there is a full professional choir of men and boys. The boys come from St Olave's Grammar School, Orpington, and receive musical training at the school as well as at the chapel. The gentlemen are all professional singers. A special feature of the services is that they all use the Book of Common Prayer, and those who love the traditional words provide the congregation.

The Master of the Music is responsible for choosing the music, training the choir and conducting the singers at the services. Although he has an assistant who plays the organ, he often plays himself. As the Chaplains come and go over the years, he takes it upon himself to see that the chapel traditions are maintained.

There is an excellent organ by Walker's, which was installed in 1965 with the Queen attending the Service of Dedication. It has given good service, and the pipes are voiced to suit the chapel. I have given a series of recitals of the works of J. S. Bach, which have been well attended and appreciated; over the years I have played the complete works: over two hundred. At the completion of this task there was an evening of celebration at the chapel.

At the conclusion of the last Royal Victorian Order Service I was taken to the Queen's private apartments at Windsor when she thanked me for all my work at the chapel and gave me a signed and dated photograph of herself and Prince Philip. With my status as Master Emeritus I am still able to advise and help over the music.

As an aside, while on the subject of the arts, I have often wondered why the Poet Laureate holds an appointment within the Royal Household, because historically there does not seem to have been a great deal of verse written in honour of the Monarch. The present Laureate, Ted Hughes, unravels the mystery quite simply: there is no commitment to the Crown whatsoever. He says: 'There is little to say about the position of Poet Laureate – a sentence would contain all of it. Wordsworth established the main condition of taking the job on: there are no duties whatsoever. It is purely an honour. If any Laureates since Wordsworth have written verses for royal occasions, it was on impulse.'

7

Lord-Lieutenants and Custos Rotulorum

Her Majesty the Queen accompanied by Lord Cottesloe, the Lord Lieutenant of Buckinghamshire, during a visit to High Wycombe in November 1994

(Photograph courtesy of Lord Cottesloe)

IT is partly because its members so frequently appear in our communities that the Royal Family remains popular in Britain. Her Majesty the Queen and other members of her family make regular visits throughout the British Isles – whether full-blown Royal Tours, official visits to open a factory, charity events or simply leisure visits. Whenever royal visitors descend for official visits, they will be closely accompanied by a smartly uniformed gentleman (or lady) who is the Queen's representative in the county. These are her Lord-

Lieutenants – one for each county — who are the most important of the Queen's representatives in the community. One of their functions is to prepare and to be of assistance during these visits, although their role involves much more besides – as anybody involved with a voluntary organization in their county will be well aware.

Commander the Lord Cottesloe, who is the Lord-Lieutenant for Buckinghamshire, served in the Royal Navy from 1945 to 1966. He was later High Sheriff of Buckinghamshire and a governor of Stowe School.

Commander the Right Honourable the Lord Cottesloe RN (ret.)
Her Majesty's Lord-Lieutenant of Buckinghamshire

Since 1984 it has been my privilege to serve as Her Majesty's Lord-Lieutenant for Buckinghamshire; that is, as the Queen's personal representative in my county. As such, it has been my very pleasant duty to receive members of the Royal Family on official visits, as well as foreign Heads of State (in my case those of France, Jordan and Nigeria). But this is not the full extent of a Lord-Lieutenant's duties. I present all sorts of medals and awards on behalf of the Sovereign (not just to individuals but also to commercial concerns, educational establishments and so on), recommend to the Lord Chancellor people suitable for appointment as Magistrates and General Commissioners and work with the armed services and in particular the reserve forces (thus perpetuating the traditional link between the Lieutenancy and the militia) and cadets.

I work, too, with all the ex-service organizations (including the Royal British Legion, of which I am County President) and support and encourage all the innumerable voluntary and charitable organizations who do such wonderful work. (Alas, they are so numerous now that I have had to draw a line to prevent my commitments becoming excessive.) Lord-Lieutenants are exhorted to promote a good atmosphere and a spirit of co-operation by encouraging voluntary service and benevolent organizations and to take an interest in the industrial and social life of the county – as Her Majesty herself does throughout the United Kingdom and the Commonwealth.

We have been honoured by several visits from Her Majesty. I particularly remember the occasion when she came to the National Centre for Epilepsy at Chalfont St Peter and the Chairman invited her to unveil the commemorative plaque. She replied, 'Aren't we going to say a prayer first?' and Bill Heseltine, her Australian Private Secretary, remarked in an aside to me, 'At least someone's read the programme.' To my mind, that incident demonstrates very clearly, albeit in a very small way, Her Majesty's meticulous and unceasing devotion to duty.

On another occasion she came to Milton's Cottage at Chalfont St Giles, which is tiny. The curator (a retired Colonel) and his wife, who was an invalid, lived in a little upstairs flat, where it had been arranged that Her Majesty would go and meet them after having tea in the marquee in the garden. As luck would have it, the Queen finished her tea and arrived at the door of the cottage just at the moment when the curator's wife had decided she was feeling better and was coming very slowly down the narrow staircase, helped by her husband. Since he had his back to the Queen, who could not get by in the very confined space, he was unaware of her presence. At a loss to know what to do, I poked the Colonel in the back with my sword scabbard to alert him to the situation. In the Navy I would probably have been required 'to give my reasons in writing' at the very least, but the Queen just turned to me with a glorious smile and said, 'It does come in useful sometimes, doesn't it, Lord-Lieutenant?'

The Queen's cousins – the 'minor royals' as they are sometimes known – may receive much unfair and misconceived criticism, but they are much in demand. My own Lieutenancy Office receives far more requests for visits from them than they can possibly fulfil (none of them is on the Civil List), but when they can come they grace every occasion by their presence and bring pride and pleasure to many.

Today's Royal Family continues a tradition of service and leadership that was first brought home to me during my wartime schooldays. I recall the magnificent example of Her Majesty's parents, who refused to send the two Princesses to Canada and safety in 1940 and refused to leave London during the Blitz (entreaties to do so after Buckingham Palace was bombed reputedly being met by the Queen with the response 'Nonsense, now I can look the East End in the face!'). Moreover, the King thwarted Winston Churchill's mad idea of being personally present on the invasion beaches in 1944 by declaring that, if the Prime Minister went, then he insisted on coming too! Such constancy earned its appropriate response. My wife, a teenage schoolgirl in London on VE Day, well remembers the enormous, good-natured throng in the Mall and its roar of 'We want the King' that brought Their Majesties on to the balcony of Buckingham Palace – eight times, I think. I shall always remember, too, serving in a destroyer of the Far East Fleet that went up the Yangtse to meet HMS *Amethyst* after she broke out of Communist Chinese incarceration. Her triumphant signal read, 'Have rejoined the Fleet south of Woosung. No damage or casualties – God Save the King.'

Our next contributor is Her Majesty's Lord-Lieutenant of Cleveland.

Lord Gisborough JP
Her Majesty's Lord-Lieutenant of Cleveland

Many people ask how a Lord-Lieutenant is selected. He is appointed by the Crown on the recommendation of the Prime Minister, who in turn takes advice from the great and the good in the county. The appointment lasts until he is seventy-five. Once appointed, the new Lord-Lieutenant may feel overwhelmed by the extreme deference paid to him by officials and others and, if he were not careful, could easily be persuaded that he had acquired instant wisdom and eminence.

First stop is the tailor, where he orders a uniform at huge cost, or he may wear his old military uniform if it is suitable. Then he must buy his sword, belt and accoutrements at even greater cost – and is mighty relieved when offered an allowance towards it all. (The need for a uniform goes back to the military origins of the office, in the reign of Henry VIII, when the holder was responsible for military matters and local defence. The militia was removed from his direct control in 1871, though he could still call out the able-bodied men of his county until 1921.)

Soon arrives notification of the first Royal Visit. The new incumbent may well have made a myriad introductions in his life, but he still rehearses every movement involved in greeting the royal guest. He must try to remember to salute, bow and call her your 'Royal Highness' and then 'Ma'am'. He must endeavour not to get so wound up that he resembles a marching cadet: trying too hard and ending up swinging the wrong arm and contorting himself with the vigour of his efforts! What light conversation should he make as they walk to the first presentations? Which side should his wife and the Chief Constable be, so that he does not fall over his sword as he presents them? And what was the name of the airport manager that rhymed with Bone?

On the day, the aircraft draws up with the Royal Standard flying over the cockpit (why does the flagstaff not puncture the aircraft's skin and ruin the pressurization?). Down comes the royal – looking at the steps as the Lord-Lieutenant salutes, so a second salute is needed as the visitor looks up. A handshake follows and hopefully the magic words of greeting; after that, of course, the visitor, like all the royals, is so charming that the Lord-Lieutenant is immediately put at his ease. (If he does make a mistake, though, no doubt it gives them a laugh on the trip back to London.)

Apart from meeting royal visitors, one of the Lord-Lieutenant's most important duties is chairing the Advisory Committee. He chooses his own committee, making sure that as far as possible every political party is represented. By advertising, coercion or any other method, the committee encourages ordinary people to apply to be magistrates and the Lord-Lieutenant or the liaison judge, with two members of the committee, interview candidates. (The office has also always been closely associated with the magistracy, and often the Lord-Lieutenant himself is an active magistrate.) Every year about 10 per cent of magistrates have to be replaced owing to retirement or other reasons, and new entrants must be found. Every effort is made to see that the magistracy represents a cross-section of society, both politically and by occupation. The committee also has to consider what to recommend to the Lord Chancellor when a justice has committed a misdemeanour, such as a motoring offence, or when one of his family may have achieved notoriety. The Lord-Lieutenant also chairs the Advisory for the Commissioners of the Inland Revenue. The Commissioners sit four or five times a year to hear tax cases, and their representative sits on the Advisory with the Lord-Lieutenant, if a meeting is called.

Another duty is to present on behalf of Her Majesty medals to those recipients who cannot travel to the Palace to receive them and also to present Queen's Awards for Industry – this often ends in a luncheon at the works. In addition, a lot of charities like the Lord-Lieutenant to be a patron or President and go to their Annual General Meetings. Also the county annual dinners of each profession – banking, insurance and so on — never seem to feel complete without the attendance of the Lord-Lieutenant.

Along with attending the Remembrance Parade, these are some of the duties carried out by the Lord-Lieutenant – with the help of a Vice-Lord-Lieutenant and Deputy Lieutenants to deputize when he cannot do a duty himself. (When he appoints new Deputies he usually selects people who have served the country or the community either in the services or through charitable work but seldom for political work.) Some Lord-Lieutenants are worked harder than others. Some have their uniform on every week, others just once or twice a year – depending on where they live and the activities of their county – but every one of them feels it is a great honour to be able to give whatever service he can in the post.

One Lieutenancy that has a particular association with the Queen is Aberdeenshire. Its current Lord-Lieutenant explains why.

Captain C. A. Farquharson of Whitehouse JP
Her Majesty's Lord-Lieutenant of Aberdeenshire

It is an enormous honour to be appointed Lord-Lieutenant of one's home county. It is an especial honour when that county is the one in which Her Majesty the Queen has her home at Balmoral Castle. This means that the Lord-Lieutenant attends a great many occasions that take place simply because of close local connections with the Royal Family. These are often low-key affairs, and they do from time to time involve quite small official engagements – such as opening the refurbished hall at Ballater or an old people's residence at Braemar. There are also the more public appearances, such as at the Braemar Games, which a house party from the Castle always attends with Her Majesty — never-to-be-forgotten occasions (even if they do take place every year) in the wonderful setting of the Princess Royal and Duke of Fife Memorial Park. When the Queen comes to Balmoral there is always an inspection of the Royal Guard at the gates of the Castle, which gives the large crowds a first opportunity to see Her Majesty on her arrival.

Aberdeenshire is a large county and to cover it requires a very considerable amount of travel every year, since there are nearly always royal visits of one kind or another to far-flung parts of the Lieutenancy.

In 1994 the Prince of Wales visited Huntly and Rhynie, a very small village that had never before had a royal visit, and the following year he honoured us with a visit to the Inverurie area. On both occasions he took the chance to meet not only young people at a playing field but also old people in a retirement home and the disabled. He was also able to see that in relatively small communities there can be both small firms and multi-million-pound businesses that export to all corners of the world. On the first visit he saw a shortbread-maker whose product is sold all over the country and beyond, next door to a building firm sending prefabricated buildings to South Africa and other countries, as well as supplying the home market. On the second occasion he saw an oil-related company doing business from China to Colombia and everywhere between; next to it was a meat-processing company meeting orders for the finest Scottish produce from the Continent, Near and Far East. These two visits not only gave His Royal Highness a chance to see how a rural county contributes to the well-being of the country, they also enabled him to meet people from small places off the beaten track – and gave them an opportunity to meet a member of the Royal Family.

Of course, these are not the only royal visits to have been made recently. The Princess Royal's visit to our Agricultural Society's 150th Show, and those by Princess Margaret to a Lighthouse Museum and the Duke of Kent to one of our very high-tech computer firms, are just a few instances of these highly appreciated occasions. The support generally is tremendous, and one comes to recognize in the crowd people who come to each and every visit, just to catch a glimpse of royalty.

The Lord-Lieutenant is actively involved in the detailed planning of a royal visit. This entails a large number of meetings with those involved on the ground and co-ordinating all the many bodies involved, such as the police and local authorities, and on some occasions involves such details as ensuring that there is a royal car available and that the menu is acceptable. The Palace representative has to be taken round the course; the timings have to be got right and everything approved.

A Lord-Lieutenant has, of course, many routine duties to perform, such as preparing the list for invitations to the royal garden parties at Buckingham Palace. He is also involved with a great many local organizations and attends their high days and some of their not-so-high days as well. Attending Guide meetings in small towns on winter evenings, or Armistice Day parades in less well-known venues, among a host of similar occasions, often involves driving along small roads with a map on one's knee, cursing one's wife for her navigational failings! However, the welcome that one receives is always so warm that it makes one appreciate what a high honour it is to be Her Majesty's Lord-Lieutenant and how great is the loyalty to the Crown in north-east Scotland.

The highlight of my time as Lord-Lieutenant has undoubtedly been the visit of Her Majesty the Queen and His Royal Highness the Duke of Edinburgh to Fraserburgh for the celebrations of the four-hundredth centenary of the Royal Burgh's Charter in 1992. The loyalty demonstrated by the crowds – six-deep on the pavements, having arrived in the early morning – was the most moving experience and, once again, showed the great popular loyalty to and love for the Royal Family.

In all this work I am, of course, enormously fortunate to have the assistance of a Clerk and Deputy Lieutenants who, among other duties, spend quite a lot of time visiting the recipients of telegrams from Her Majesty on important anniversaries and also representing the Lieutenancy from time to time and at Armistice ceremonies. They help with the lists of names for the garden parties, with royal visits and act as sounding-boards for the community in their areas and generally help by keeping one in touch. Quite apart from all the official assistance, there is also the unstinted support of my wife, whose efforts make it possible for me to represent Her Majesty in this way.

Henry Elwes, Her Majesty's Lord-Lieutenant of Gloucestershire, a former Scots Guards officer, explains something of the appointment's military origin and illuminates the position of Custos Rotulorum.

Henry Elwes JP
Her Majesty's Lord-Lieutenant of Gloucestershire

I was appointed Lord-Lieutenant of Gloucestershire by Her Majesty in much the same way that Bishops are appointed; that is, on the recommendation of the Prime Minister and after local consultation. The post was created in the sixteenth century and is military in origin, going back to the time when the job of raising the county's volunteer forces was taken from the High Sheriff. Until fairly recently, therefore, it was normal for Lord-Lieutenants to have had a distinguished career in either the regular or territorial forces.

Today the Lord-Lieutenant still maintains close links with the regular, territorial and cadet forces, but as the Queen's personal representative his major responsibility is to organize all royal visits to the county. In Gloucestershire we have twenty to thirty such visits each year. Each one is an exciting occasion on which those who help to make the county function, or who need special support, are invariably stimulated by the genuine interest that all members of the Royal Family show in their affairs.

In addition to this, a Lord-Lieutenant may be Custos Rotulorum (Keeper of the Rolls), one of the oldest of all offices. This places him at the head of the county's lay justices and makes him chairman of the Advisory Committee. In this post he will be responsible, in conjunction with the Lord Chancellor, for maintaining the strength and standing of the magistracy.

Finally the Lord-Lieutenant offers support and encouragement to local authorities and services, the business community and the many volunteers who do so much to ensure the well-being of his county. He will be asked to present awards, medals and certificates, both those awarded by the Queen and the many of local origin. He will also attend most of the important functions in his county, often speaking on appropriate occasions.

For all royal visits and other formal occasions, such as parades, processions and presentations, he will normally wear uniform with sword and will usually take a smart young cadet to act as ADC for the day. To assist with the workload there will be a Vice-Lord-Lieutenant, and a number of Deputies can be called upon from time to time as well. It is a busy job, but it is an enormous privilege and honour to represent Her Majesty and the county. Sometimes there are a few good laughs on the way home too!

Lord-Lieutenants are assisted by Vice-Lord-Lieutenants and Deputy Lieutenants. General Sir David Fraser, Vice-Lord-Lieutenant of Hampshire, previously served in the Grenadier Guards and was ADC General to Her Majesty the Queen, as well as Colonel of the Royal Hampshire Regiment.

General Sir David Fraser GCB OBE DL
ADC General to the Queen, 1977 – 1980
Her Majesty's Vice-Lord-Lieutenant of Hampshire

The Lord-Lieutenant of a county is appointed by Her Majesty the Queen. A number of Deputy Lieutenants – the number for each county is fixed by a formula relating to its size and population – may also be selected, and the Lord-Lieutenant may appoint one of them as Vice-Lord-Lieutenant, subject to Her Majesty's approval. I was appointed Vice-Lord-Lieutenant of the County of Hampshire in 1988 by Sir James Scott, who died in 1993, and his successor, Mrs Fagan, appointed me in 1994. (The appointment of Vice-Lord-Lieutenant lapses when the Lord-Lieutenant who appointed him dies or resigns.)

In my capacity as Vice-Lord-Lieutenant I have frequently had the pleasurable duty of meeting the Queen and other members of the Royal Family, making presentations, accompanying them throughout their visits and taking leave at their conclusion. From this a number of impressions – all widely familiar – will always remain. First, there is the Queen's interest and information. Well briefed, Her Majesty invariably shows expert, flattering interest in whatever she is being shown or whoever is presented to her. To appear genuinely concerned and absorbed by the many thousands of different people and activities she encounters each year – to give to each person the feeling that her interest is not mechanical but personal and authentic – is a wonderful gift. And nobody, surely, should underestimate how exhausting it must be to display such a gift so often and for so long.

My second impression is of the high standards the Queen invariably expects. The slightest deviation from what has been planned and approved, the smallest imperfection in arrangements that should be perfect, is unlikely to go unremarked. As anybody who has been close to her on military occasions knows well, Her Majesty has the eye of a great Commanding Officer, and her attention to detail is legendary. Only unwise officers of a Lieutenancy will fail to check and scrutinize every aspect of a Royal Visit.

This may sound formidable, and in a sense it should. But my third and ineffaceable impression is of the simple happiness that the Queen's visits and presence produce. Her smile, her charm, her kindness, her sympathetic interest in the activities or concerns or personalities covered by a Royal Visit spread warmth and light. The Queen knows well that in one person's life there may only be one moment of direct speech or contact with their Sovereign, and she knows well, too, how to make that moment memorable. To witness this has been a privilege indeed.

We often hear how members of the Royal Family pay particular attention to local and national charitable organizations – perhaps the most famous pairing being that of the Princess Royal and the Save the Children Fund. Lord Rix (better known to millions as Brian Rix the comic actor and farceur) is both Her Majesty's Vice-Lord-Lieutenant of Greater London and the chairman of Mencap. Here he stresses the importance of Royal Patronage to British charity. The members of the Royal Family are patrons, presidents and chairmen of dozens of charities, large and small, and the good achieved through their association is incalculable. Lord Rix speaks not only for Mencap, I am sure, but also for the countless other organizations that share in this benevolence.

The Right Honourable Lord Rix CBE DL
Chairman of Mencap
Her Majesty's Vice-Lord-Lieutenant of Greater London

I am delighted to be able to draw attention to the special relationship between the Royal Family and the voluntary sector. Since 1946 Mencap has grown to become the UK's largest voluntary organization for people with learning disabilities and their families, a powerful, pioneering and campaigning organization. The passing of its fiftieth anniversary provides a fitting opportunity to look at the part the Royal Family have played, and the milestones they have marked, in the history of the organization.

Initially there were separate Royal and National Societies for Mentally Handicapped Children and Adults. In 1962 the Queen Mother became Patron of the Royal Society. A year later she opened

The Lord Rix, with her Majesty Queen Elizabeth the Queen Mother, Royal Patron of Mencap, at the opening of the Mencap National Centre in December 1981

(Photograph copyright London Borough of Islington – Libraries Department; reproduced with permission)

the National Society's newly built hostel and training workshop in Slough (the first training centre for adults with learning disabilities and a dream come true for many members). Mencap's links with royalty were cemented in 1981 when the National Society was amalgamated into the Royal Society, and on 10 December of the same year the Queen Mother opened Mencap's National Centre in Golden Lane – our present headquarters. In 1986 – the year of the first major legislation for people with learning disabilities – Mencap celebrated its fortieth anniversary and the twenty-fifth year of the Queen Mother's patronage. She graciously helped to mark the occasion by being a guest of honour at a special reception at St James's Palace. It was attended by a record number of Mencap members and their families, and the Queen Mother spent an inordinate amount of time talking to the guests.

As we approach the millennium, Mencap can now proudly stand as one of the top charities in the voluntary sector. When the Queen

Mother generously associated herself with the charity in the 1960s it was relatively unknown, and the fact that today it is ranked among the top twenty charities owes a very great deal to her patronage and generosity over the years.

As well as Lord-Lieutenants and their Deputies, certain other individuals are sometimes involved with royal visits to local or regional communities. An MP may be involved in a visit to his constituency or a minister in one to region or project for which he is responsible. Indeed a Secretary of State – who is both an MP and (as Sir Edward Ford explained earlier) one of Her Majesty's official advisers – may have dealings with royalty at local, regional or national level.

Tom King, MP for Bridgwater and Secretary of State in a number of departments (latterly Northern Ireland and Defence), recalls some of the moments during his political career that brought him into direct contact with the Royal Family.

The Right Honourable Tom King CH MP
Secretary of State for Defence (1989 – 1992)
Secretary of State for Northern Ireland (1985 – 1989)

It is one of the privileges of a Secretary of State for Northern Ireland, and also a Secretary of State for Defence, to be closely involved with Her Majesty and the Royal Family in a whole range of different activities. They may be ceremonial. They may be quite informal, like meeting members of a crowd during a visit. There may be moments of intimate personal grief, such as the visit of the Prince of Wales to console the families after a bomb outrage in Northern Ireland.

At all times I have been enormously affected by the warmth and enthusiasm of the reception that members of the Royal Family have received. You only have to look into the eyes of the crowds and the people to whom they might be talking to see the strength of our Monarchy and the indispensable role that it plays in the hearts of so many in our country. Her Majesty the Queen's outstanding record of service and devotion to our country is recognized by all, and the Prince of Wales, in his own distinctive style, has brought so much to so many people through his wide range of interests.

I shall never forget the experience of accompanying Queen Elizabeth the Queen Mother at the special parade organized by the Ministry of Defence to pay tribute to her on her ninetieth birthday. In the presence of Her Majesty the Queen and many members of the Royal Family, the spotlight shone on the remarkable life of service to her country of that most loved of figures, Her Majesty the Queen Mother. The response of the thousands taking part in the parade – the huge audience in Horse Guards Parade and, more widely, on television – left no possible doubt of the deep affection that so many feel for the Monarchy and the vital part it plays in our nation.

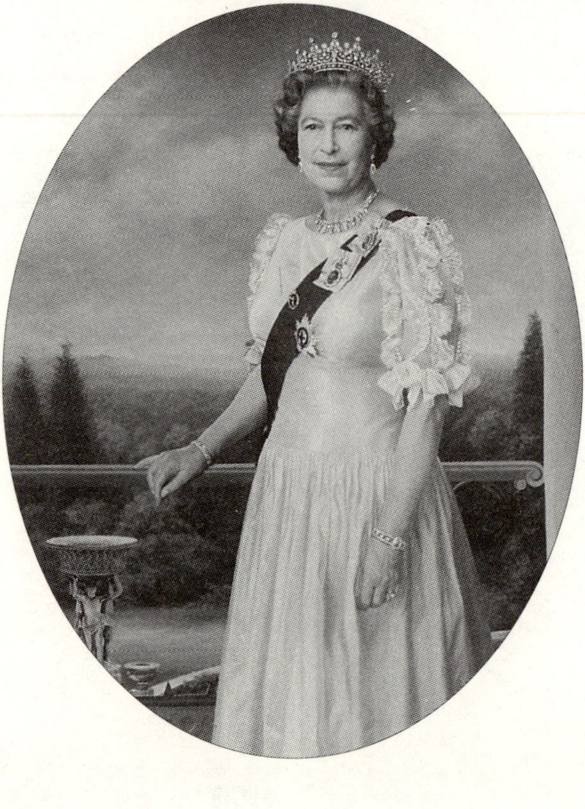